THE BOOK OF
PRESERVES
JAMS · CHUTNEYS · PICKLES · JELLIES

THE BOOK OF PRESERVES

JAMS · CHUTNEYS · PICKLES · JELLIES

MARY NORWAK

Photography by JON STEWART

GOLDEN PRESS
SYDNEY · AUCKLAND

Published 1986 by Golden Press Pty Limited
5-01 Henry Lawson Business Centre, Birkenhead
Point, Drummoyne, N.S.W. 2047, Australia, and
16 Copsey Place, Avondale, Auckland, New Zealand.

By arrangement with Merehurst Press
5 Great James Street, London, WC1N 3DA
©Copyright Merehurst Limited 1986

ISBN 0 7302 03964

Editors: Hilary Walden, Chris Fayers
Designers: Roger Daniels, Richard Slater, Stuart Willard
Food stylist: Barbara Stewart
Photographer: Jon Stewart
Typeset by Lineage
Colour separation and printing by New Interlitho S.p.A., Milan

ACKNOWLEDGEMENTS
The publishers would like to thank the following for their help and advice:
David Mellor, 4 Sloane Square, London SW1W 8EE, telephone 01-730-4259
David Mellor, 26 James Street, Covent Garden, London WC2E 8PA, telephone
01-379-6947
David Mellor, 66 King Street, Manchester M2 4NP, telephone 061-834-7023
Elizabeth David Limited, 46 Bourne Street, London SW1, telephone 01-730-3123
and at Covent Garden Kitchen Supplies, 3 North Row, The Market, London WC2,
telephone 01-836-9167
Harrods Limited, Knightsbridge, London SW1, telephone 01-730-1234
Phillips Home Appliances, City House, 420-430 London Road, Croydon, CR9
3QR, telephone 01-689-2166
Lakeland Plastics, Alexandra Building, Windermere, Cumbria, LA23 1BQ

Companion volumes of interest:
The Book of GARNISHES
The Book of COCKTAILS
The Book of CHOCOLATES AND PETITS FOURS
The Book of HORS D'OEUVRES
The Book of SAUCES
The Book of ICE CREAMS AND SORBETS
The Book of GIFTS FROM THE PANTRY

CONTENTS

THE BOOK OF

——————— INTRODUCTION ———————

Preserving is one of the oldest and most satisfying forms of cooking. For hundreds of years, cooks have enjoyed preparing their bounty of summer fruit and vegetables in a variety of ways in order to prepare delicious meals during the less plentiful days of winter.

Until partway through the 20th century, a country household aimed to be totally self-sufficient, drying fruit, vegetables and herbs, preparing pickles, chutneys and sauces and making jams and other delicious sweet preserves. Candying fruit, making liqueurs or bottling fruit in alcohol were activities of more leisured homemakers who could afford time and a little extra money for preserving their fruits.

Today, freezers deal with bulky supplies, but preserving is such a satisfying activity that many people enjoy it as a leisure pastime. Additionally, there is now a strong feeling for old-fashioned ways of past years and for the nostalgic delicacies which so delighted our ancestors. While families obviously enjoy results, cooks get great pleasure from offering specialities as gifts. Presentation is almost as important as initial preparation.

In this book, recipes are provided for unusual preserves which are not difficult to prepare, will give a special touch to everyday meals and will make delightful and welcome presents for all occasions.

UTENSILS

Equipment for preserving is not expensive or difficult to obtain. Many items are already in household use. It is important to use correct utensils to ensure good results.

Large, heavy-based saucepan or preserving pan is essential so preserves containing sugar do not burn. A pan should be large so jam may be boiled hard without boiling over and wide enough to allow rapid evaporation of liquid to aid setting. A true preserving pan does not have a long handle, which could be dangerous, but is fitted with a pair of short looped handles, or a bail (a carrying handle over the top). A suitable saucepan may be used if necessary. A pan should be made of aluminium or stainless steel. Copper will help to keep green fruits green, but will spoil the colour of red fruit. Chipped enamel can be dangerous, while zinc or iron can spoil colour or flavour.

Long handled wooden spoon is necessary as preserves are very hot and hands should be well away from danger of splashing.

Strainer or sieve is useful when preparing purées. It should have a non-metallic mesh to prevent discolouration.

Kitchen scales or measuring jugs are needed, as correct proportions of ingredients are necessary for success. Careful weighing or measuring is important.

Large mixing bowl is needed, particularly for preparing pickles and chutneys. Choose one made of ovenglass, earthenware or stainless steel.

Sugar thermometer is useful to check setting point of preserves, jams and jellies.

Jam funnel is a small inexpensive item which is useful for helping to keep jars clean when filling.

Jelly bag is necessary for preparing jellies and syrups. It is suspended from its own stand. If not available, a piece of muslin may be used instead.

Stainless steel slotted spoon is useful for removing scum from jams and jellies, and also lifting and draining solid ingredients which must be packed into jars.

Jars may be new or used and should be scrupulously clean. Screwtop or clip jars are useful for many preserves. Lids need vinegar-proof linings for pickles, chutneys and sauces.

Jars for herbs should be small and made of dark glass to prevent penetration of light and fading of contents.

INGREDIENTS

Fruit

Choose fresh and firm, not mushy fruit. It should be slightly under-ripe. Very ripe fruit has reduced sugar content which will affect setting and quality. Sort fruit carefully and discard any bruised or damaged pieces. If fruit needs to be washed, with the exception of berries, place in a sieve or colander under cold running water and carefully dry. Wash fruit low in pectin, such as strawberries, as little as possible. Remove the stones or peel fruit with stainless steel or silver kitchen tools to prevent discolouration. Prepare fruit immediately before cooking or fruit will deteriorate.

Vegetables

For pickles and chutneys, vegetables should be ready for eating. Do not choose over-mature vegetables or they become tough and stringy. Wash well and dry, then peel or otherwise prepare as necessary. As with fruit, prepare immediately before use.

Dried Fruit

All dried fruit should be plump, fresh and of high quality. If washing is necessary, place fruit in a sieve or colander and rinse under cold running water. Dry completely before using.

Sugar

Granulated sugar may be used for all preserves. Brown sugars are often used to give colour and flavour to pickles, chutneys and sauces. They do not give a good set to sweet preserves, although the flavour is delicious. Honey also gives a good flavour but prevents firm setting.

Dissolve sugar slowly and carefully in preserves by heating gently and stirring occasionally. If sugar crystals remain undissolved, they may burn on the bottom of the pan, and affect smoothness of finished product. Warm sugar slightly in a warm oven before adding to fruit, and it will dissolve more quickly.

Vinegar

Use vinegar of good quality and containing at least 5% acetic acid or it will not preserve fruit or vegetables. Malt vinegar has a strong flavour and colour. White vinegar is preferable for clear pickles and spiced fruit although the flavour is very strong. Wine vinegar and cider vinegar give a better flavour to more delicate preserves. Ready-spiced vinegar may be purchased. More individual flavours can be achieved by using whole spices infused in warm vinegar.

Acid

Lemon juice, citric or tartaric acid are added to some fruits before cooking to extract pectin, improve colour and prevent crystallization. To 1.8 kg (4 lb.) fruit, allow 2 tablespoons lemon juice or ½ teaspoon citric or tartaric acid.

Pectin

The pectin content of fruit affects setting quality of jams and jellies. Fruits with *High Pectin Content* include apples, blackcurrants, damsons, gooseberries, plums and redcurrants. *Medium Pectin Content* fruits include apricots, early blackberries, greengages and loganberries. *Low Pectin Content* fruits include late blackberries, cherries, pears, rhubarb, raspberries, strawberries and tomatoes. Pips and pith of fruit contain pectin and are sometimes cooked with fruit. Pectin may be introduced into a preserve with a mixture of fruit, such as apples with blackberries. Commercial pectin may be added to preserves. Follow manufacturers' instructions carefully.

Spices

Use fresh and fragrant spices or a musty flavour will develop. Whole spices are usually tied into a muslin bag and suspended in pan during preparation and then discarded. A few whole spices may be included in some preserves to give a stronger flavour during maturation and to give an attractive appearance.

SETTING, PACKING AND SEALING PRESERVES

Setting Tests

A preserve for storage needs 60% added sugar content, or 3 parts sugar to 5 parts preserve. Some preserves are ready for setting after boiling rapidly 5 minutes while others need to boil rapidly 20 minutes. Make setting tests at 5 minute intervals. If a preserve is boiled too long, it will never set. When preserve reaches setting point, remove from heat at once. There are three setting tests:

a) **Temperature test** – dip a sugar thermometer in hot water. Stir preserve and submerge the thermometer bulb completely in preserve. When thermometer registers 105C (221F), the preserve is ready.

b) **Plate test** – pour a small amount of preserve on a cold plate. Let stand until cold. If preserve forms a skin and wrinkles when pushed with a finger, it is ready. Remove pan from the heat while test preserve is cooling.

c) **Sheeting test** – dip a chilled spoon in the boiling preserve. Let preserve drip from the spoon. When preserve no longer falls off spoon in drips but in a sheet preserve is ready.

Packing

Wash jars in hot, soapy water; rinse. After washing, plunge jars into boiling water. Dry in a warm oven. Handle as little as possible.

When preserve is ready, remove pan from heat. If preserve contains solid fruit or peel, let stand 5 to 10 minutes. Stir preserve gently so fruit will not rise in jars. Ladle hot preserve into jars, using a jam funnel fitted into neck of jar. Fill jar to the top. Tap jar gently to release air bubbles.

Sealing

Wipe rim of jar with a clean damp cloth. Place waxed disc on top of preserve; cover with snap-on lid, screwtop or cellophane. If cellophane is used, dip in water, place tightly over top of jar to become slightly concave and airtight, secure with rubber band or string.

Storage

Do not move until preserve is firmly set. Store in a cool, dry, dark place.

PACKAGING

Jars or bottles

Choose a container which is suitable for contents. Pickles and chutneys look inviting in professional preserving jars with screwtop or clip-on lids. If made for a gift, they might be packaged in an antique or modern pickle jar ready for a table. Expensive conserves look very special in decorative and unusually shaped jars rather than traditional straight-sided jars. Jellies are often needed in small quantities for one-meal servings, and can be ladled into small jars. Curds can be placed in small bowls.

Vinegars can be bottled in flasks ready for a table, and mustards in jars which can go straight on a condiment tray. Liqueurs can be bottled in traditional bottles. A small quantity for a gift might be decanted into an individual flask.

Cleanliness

While containers have been cleaned and sterilized before use, they can become messy during preparation and filling. While still hot, containers can be wiped with a soft cloth dipped in warm water and detergent, and carefully dried. When contents are cold, polish jars with a cloth dipped in methylated spirit.

Labels

All preserves should be clearly and informatively labelled. Labels should be clean, neat, carefully written, and applied on container.

Covers

All preserves must be firmly and tightly sealed, but tops of jars are not always sightly. Use polished or coloured metal or plastic tops without identification. If trade-names are on reused containers, paint with enamel or cover with a circle of stick-on plastic fabric.

A most attractive finishing touch can be made by tying a thin string or decorative tape or ribbon around a paper or cotton fabric topping. For a special effect, cut paper or fabric with pinking shears. Use cheerful bold checked or plain fabric for pickles, chutneys or everyday sweet preserves, and very pretty patterns for conserves, curds or fruit in alcohol.

Presentation Gifts

A collection of preserves or a single jar or bottle can make a very attractive gift, but it is pleasant to give something extra to make a present memorable. Five single jars of jam in a box covered with pretty paper or foil, together with a little jam dish or a spoon, or give a flask of liqueur with a suitable glass or a jar of conserve or fruit in alcohol with a serving bowl or a jar of cream.

If a number of jars are packaged together, try to vary coverings to make a more interesting collection. Again, add a suitable complementary item such as a wedge of cheese with two or three pickles, or a serving tray to hold a variety of preserves.

A strong box neatly covered with pretty wrapping paper or foil makes a good container. Crumpled paper or polythene granules keep glass and bottles safe. Baskets look good, or items such as a new pan, colander or serving tray. Finish the gift with plenty of ribbons and an attractive gift card.

LABELLING

Clearly written labels are essential to identify all types of preserves. They may be decorative as well as informative. Labels for each batch of jars or bottles should be identical, so they are easily recognized. Labels should be clean and unwrinkled, and applied neatly on jars. Write in water-proof ink, never in pencil so label remains clear. Some suggestions for making your own labels are shown in the picture below, and add these relevant details

a) *Name of preserve*
If preserve is traditionally known as something like "Anna's Special Jelly", add main flavouring ingredients.
b) *Date of preparation*
This is final date of packaging, sealing and labelling.
c) *Eat-by date*
In case of short-life preparations such as Lemon Curd, this should be date after which preserve becomes unattractive or inedible. Pickles and chutneys can have a maturity date after which they will be excellent to eat.
d) *Special Notes*
This need only be indicated on unfamiliar preserves, not on basic jams, to tell recipient best ways of using contents.

JAMS

Jam is made of fruits or fruit juices, pectin, acid and sugar. It is less firm than jelly. Fruits, such as apples, plums, lemons, limes and oranges, are high in pectin content, which, when combined with sugar helps jam to set. Strawberries, cherries and peaches are low in pectin content, and lemon juice is often added to these fruits to aid setting and bring out the flavour of the fruit.

Use sound, slightly under-ripe fruit which is not mushy. Wash and dry. Remove stems, leaves and any bruised parts. Prepare fruit according to recipe.

In a large saucepan, simmer fruit and water until fruit is soft and mixture is reduced by ½.

Add sugar. Stir until sugar dissolves.

Increase heat. Bring to a boil. Boil rapidly until jam reaches 105C (221F).

Remove from heat. Test for setting. Cool a small amount of jam on a cool plate 1 minute. Push with a finger to form wrinkles.

Skim jam to remove scum. Cool 5 to 10 minutes. Stir well. Ladle hot jam into hot jars; cover and label.

Plum and Cherry Brandy Jam

1.4 kg (3 lb.) plums, stoned, coarsely chopped

125 ml (5 fl oz/²⁄₃ cup) water

8 tablespoons lemon juice

1.6 kg (3½ lb./8 cups) sugar

4 tablespoons cherry brandy

Wash 6 (450 g/16 oz) jars in hot, soapy water; rinse. Keep hot until needed.

In a large saucepan, cook plums and water over low heat until plums are very soft. Add lemon juice. Simmer 5 minutes. Add sugar. Stir until sugar dissolves. Increase heat; boil rapidly for 15 minutes or until jam reaches 105C (221F).

Remove from heat. Stir in cherry brandy. Remove scum. Let stand 5 minutes.

Stir well. Ladle hot jam into 1 hot jar at a time. Wipe rim of jar with a clean damp cloth. Cover. Fill and cover remaining jars.

Makes 6 (450 g)16 oz).

Peach and Raspberry Jam

1 kg (2 lb.) peaches, peeled, sliced

155 ml (5 fl oz/⅔ cup) water

2 tablespoons lemon juice

1 kg (2 lb./6⅓ cups) raspberries, stems removed

1.4 kg (3lb./6¾ cups) sugar

Wash 5 (450 g/16 oz) jars in hot, soapy water; rinse. Keep hot until needed.

In a large saucepan, simmer peaches, water and lemon juice until peaches are soft. Add raspberries. Simmer 5 minutes. Add sugar. Stir until sugar dissolves. Increase heat; boil rapidly 15 to 20 minutes until jam reaches 105C (221F). Remove from heat. Remove scum. Cool 5 to 10 minutes.

Ladle hot jam into 1 hot jar at a time. Wipe rim of jar with a clean damp cloth. Cover. Fill and cover remaining jars.

Makes 5 (450 g/16 oz).

Rhubarb and Angelica Jam

1.8 kg (4 lb.) rhubarb, cut in 2.5-cm (1-in) pieces

1.4 kg (3lb./6¾ cups) sugar

½ teaspoon citric acid

250 g (8 oz/1¼ cup) chopped crystallized angelica

In a large bowl, alternate layers of rhubarb and sugar. Let stand in a cool place 24 hours.

Wash 5 (450 g/16 oz) jars in hot, soapy water; rinse. Keep hot until needed.   In a large saucepan, bring rhubarb, sugar and citric acid to a boil, stirring continuously. Reduce heat; simmer 10 minutes. Increase heat; boil rapidly 10 minutes or until jam reaches 105C (221F).

Remove from heat. Stir in angelica. Remove scum. Let stand 5 minutes.

Stir well. Ladle hot jam into 1 hot jar at a time. Wipe rim of jar with a clean damp cloth. Cover. Fill and cover remaining jars.

Makes 5 (450 g/16 oz).

Pear and Peach Jam

1 kg (2 lb.) ripe pears

750 g (1½ lb.) peaches, peeled, sliced, stoned

125 ml (5 fl oz/²⁄₃ cup) water

1.4 kg (3 lb./6¾) cups sugar

Grated peel and juice of 3 lemons

Wash 5 (450 g/16 oz) jars in hot, soapy water; rinse. Keep hot until needed.

Peel and core pears; tie cores in a muslin bag. Chop flesh.

In a large saucepan bring pears, muslin bag, peaches and water to a boil. Reduce heat; simmer until fruit is soft. Discard muslin bag. Add sugar, lemon peel and juice. Stir until sugar dissolves. Increase heat; boil rapidly 15 to 20 minutes or until jam reaches 105C (221F). Remove from heat. Remove scum. Cool 5 to 10 minutes.

Ladle hot jam into 1 hot jar at a time. Wipe rim of jar with a clean damp cloth. Cover. Fill and cover remaining jars.

Makes 5 (450 g/16 oz).

Apricot and Date Low Sugar Jam

450 g (1 lb./3 cups) dried apricots

1.1 l (2 pt/5 cups) water

750 g (1½ lb./4½ cups) dates, chopped

250 g (8 oz/1 cup) sugar

Juice of 1 lemon

60 g (2 oz/½ cup) almonds, chopped

In a large bowl combine apricots and ½ of water. Let stand 12 hours.
   Wash 5 (250 g/8 oz) jars in hot, soapy water; rinse. Keep hot until
needed. In a large saucepan, simmer apricots and liquid, remaining
water and dates until apricots are soft. Add sugar and lemon juice.
Stir until sugar dissolves. Simmer until jam thickens; stir in almonds.
Cook 2 minutes. Remove from heat. Remove scum. Cool 5 to 10
minutes.
   Ladle hot jam into 1 hot jar at a time. Wipe rim of jar with a clean
damp cloth. Cover. Fill and cover remaining jars.

Makes 5 (250 g/8 oz).

Apple Ginger Jam

1.4 kg (3 lb.) cooking apples, peeled, cored, thinly sliced

600 ml (1 pt/2½ cups) water

Grated peel and juice of 2 lemons

1 teaspoon ground ginger

1.4 kg (3 lb./6¾ cups) sugar

125 g (4 oz/½ cup) chopped crystallized ginger

Wash 5 (450 g/16 oz) jars in hot, soapy water; rinse. Keep hot until needed.

In a large saucepan, simmer apples, water, lemon peel and juice and ground ginger until apples are soft. Add sugar. Stir until sugar dissolves. Increase heat; boil rapidly 15 to 20 minutes or until jam reaches 105C (221F). Remove from heat. Stir in crystallized ginger. Remove scum. Let stand for 5 to 10 minutes.

Ladle hot jam into 1 hot jar at a time. Wipe rim of jar with a clean damp cloth. Cover. Fill and cover remaining jars.

Makes 5 (450 g/16 oz).

Fruit Salad Jam

450 g (1 lb./3 cups) dried fruit salad (apples, pears, apricots,prunes) coarsely chopped

1.7 l (3 pt/7½ cups) water

3 tablespoons lemon juice

1.4 kg (3 lb./6¾ cups) sugar

In a large bowl, combine fruit salad and water. Let stand 24 hours.

Wash 5 (450 g/16 oz) jars in hot, soapy water; rinse. Keep hot until needed.

In a large saucepan, simmer fruit salad and liquid 40 minutes. Add lemon juice and sugar. Stir until sugar dissolves. Increase heat; boil rapidly 15 to 20 minutes or until jam reaches 105C (221F).

Remove from heat. Remove scum. Let stand 5 minutes.

Ladle hot jam into 1 hot jar at a time. Wipe rim of jar with a clean damp cloth. Cover. Fill and cover remaining jars.

Makes 5 (450 g/16 oz).

Strawberry Jam

1.6 kg (3½ lb.) strawberries, hulled

3 tablespoons lemon juice

1.4 kg (3 lb./6 cups) sugar

Wash 5 (450 g/16 oz.) jars in hot, soapy water; rinse. Keep hot until needed.

In a large saucepan, simmer strawberries and lemon juice 30 minutes or until strawberries are soft. Add sugar. Stir until sugar dissolves. Increase heat; boil rapidly 15 to 20 minutes or until jam reaches 105C (221F).

Remove from heat. Remove scum. Let stand 15 minutes.

Stir well. Ladle hot jam into 1 hot jar at a time. Wipe rim of jar with a clean damp cloth. Cover. Fill and cover remaining jars.

Makes 5 (450 g/16 oz).

Rose Petal Jam

450 g (1 lb.) dark red rose petals

750 g (1½ lb./3½ cups) sugar

310 ml (10 fl oz/1¼ cups) water

1 tablespoon lemon juice

3 tablespoons rosewater

Snip white bottoms from rose petals; discard. Chop petals coarsely. In a large bowl, combine chopped petals and ½ of sugar. Let stand, covered, 48 hours.

Wash 3 (250 g/8 oz) jars in hot soapy water; rinse. Keep hot until needed. In a large saucepan, cook water, lemon juice and remaining sugar over low heat until sugar dissolves, stirring continuously. Add rose petals and liquid. Increase heat; boil rapidly 20 minutes.

Remove from heat. Stir in rosewater. Remove scum. Let stand 5 to 10 minutes.

Ladle hot jam into 1 hot jar at a time. Wipe rim of jar with a clean damp cloth. Cover. Fill and cover remaining jars.

Jam has a thick syrup consistency.

Makes 3 (250 g/8 oz).

Dried Apricot and Pear Jam

450 g (1 lb./3 cups) dried apricots

600 ml (1 pt/2½ cups) water

1.4 kg (3 lb.) ripe pears, peeled, coarsely chopped

4 tablespoons lemon juice

1.6 kg (3½ lb./7 cups) sugar

**3 tablespoons apricot brandy, Grand Marnier
or Curaçao, if desired**

In a large bowl combine apricots and water. Let stand 12 hours.
Wash 6 (450 g/16 oz) jars in hot, soapy water; rinse. Keep hot until needed. In a large saucepan, simmer apricots, liquid, pears and lemon juice 20 minutes. Add sugar. Stir until sugar dissolves. Increase heat; boil rapidly 15 to 20 minutes until jam reaches 105C (221F).

Remove from heat. Stir in apricot brandy, Grand Marnier or Curaçao, if desired. Remove scum. Let stand 5 to 10 minutes.

Ladle hot jam into 1 hot jar at a time. Wipe rim of jar with a clean damp cloth. Cover. Fill and cover remaining jars.

Makes 6 (450 g/16 oz).

Black Cherry Jam

1.8 kg (4 lb.) black cherries,

1 teaspoon citric acid

1.6 kg (3½ lb/8 cups) sugar

Remove stones from cherries; crack stones, remove kernels. Wash 6 (450 g/16 oz) jars in hot soapy water; rinse. Keep hot until needed.

In a large saucepan, cook cherries, kernels and citric acid over low heat until cherries are very soft. Stir often. Add sugar. Stir until sugar dissolves. Increase heat; boil rapidly 20 minutes or until jam reaches 105C (221F). Remove from heat. Remove scum. Cool 5 to 10 minutes.

Ladle hot jam into 1 hot jar at a time. Wipe rim of jar with a clean damp cloth. Cover lid. Fill and cover remaining jars.

Makes 6 (450 g/16 oz)

Kiwifruit Jam

1 kg (2 lb.) kiwifruit, peeled, chopped

½ teaspoon citric acid

750 g (1½ lb./3½ cups) sugar

Wash 3 (250 g/8 oz) jars in hot, soapy water; rinse. Keep hot until needed.

In a large saucepan, cook kiwifruit and citric acid over low heat until kiwifruit is soft. Add sugar. Stir until sugar dissolves. Increase heat, boil rapidly 10 minutes or until jam reaches 105C (221F). Remove from heat. Remove scum. Cool 5 to 10 minutes.

Ladle hot jam into 1 hot jar at a time. Wipe rim of jar with a clean damp cloth. Cover. Fill and cover remaining jars.

Makes 3 (250 g (8 oz).

Orange Jam

1.4 kg (3 lb.) Valencia oranges, thinly sliced

Pinch of salt

750 g (1½ lb/3½ cups) sugar

1.7 l (3 pt/7½ cups) water

Remove pips but not peel from orange slices. Tie pips in a muslin bag; set aside.

In a large bowl, cover orange slices with water. Let stand 48 hours. Change water 3 times. Drain; discard liquid.

Wash 5 (250 g/8 oz) jars in hot, soapy water; rinse. Keep hot until needed.

In a large saucepan, cover orange slices with water. Add salt. Cook over low heat until orange slices are transparent. Drain; discard liquid.

In a large saucepan, cook sugar and 1.7 l (3 pt./7½ cups) water over low heat until sugar dissolves, stirring continuously. Increase heat; boil 10 minutes. Add orange slices and bag of pips. Bring to a boil again. Reduce heat; simmer 30 minutes. Remove from heat. Discard bag of pips. Remove scum. Cool 5 to 10 minutes.

Ladle hot jam into 1 hot jar at a time. Wipe rim of jar with a clean damp cloth. Cover. Fill and cover remaining jars.

Jam is runny.

Makes 5 (250 g/8 oz).

Four Fruit Jam

250 g (8 oz/2 cups) blackcurrants, stems removed

3 tablespoons water

250 g (8 oz/2 cups) redcurrants, stems removed

250 g (8 oz/1½ cups) raspberries, stems removed

250 g (8 oz/1¼ cups) strawberries, hulled

900 g (2 lb./4 cups) sugar

Wash 6 (250 g/8 oz) jars in hot, soapy water; rinse. Keep hot until needed.

In a large saucepan, cook blackcurrants and water over low heat until blackcurrants are soft. Add redcurrants, raspberries, and strawberries. Cook 10 minutes. Add sugar. Stir until sugar dissolves. Increase heat; boil rapidly 10 to 15 minutes or until jam reaches 105C (221F). Remove from heat. Remove scum. Cool 5 to 10 minutes.

Ladle hot jam into 1 hot jar at a time. Wipe rim of jar with a clean damp cloth. Cover. Fill and cover remaining jars.

Makes 6 (250 g/8 oz).

JELLIES

A quality jelly is clear and sparkling. It should retain its shape and quiver if removed from its jar. A good set depends upon the presence of sugar, pectin and acid in correct proportions. Follow the recipe carefully. Do not be tempted to hasten jelly making by squeezing the jelly bag or the result will be a cloudy jelly. Use as a spread on toast, bread, sweet rolls or muffins or as an accompaniment with meats.

Use sound, slightly under-ripe fruit which is not mushy. Wash and dry. Remove stems, leaves and any bruised parts. Prepare fruit according to recipe.

In a large saucepan, cook fruit and water, if necessary, over low heat until fruit is very soft.

Suspend a jelly bag over a large bowl. Pour mixture into jelly bag. Allow juice to drip slowly. Do not squeeze, stir or shake bag or jelly will be cloudy.

Measure juice. Weigh recommended quantity of sugar in proportion to juice.

In a large saucepan, warm juice. Add sugar. Cook over low heat, until sugar dissolves. Stir occasionally.

Increase heat. Boil rapidly until jelly reaches 105C (221F). Remove from heat. Remove scum. Ladle hot jelly into hot jars. Cover.

Orange and Apple Jelly

4 oranges, coarsely chopped

1.4 kg (3 lb.) cooking apples, coarsely chopped

1.7l (3 pts/7½ cups) water

Sugar

In a large saucepan, simmer oranges, apples and water 1½ hours or until orange peel is very soft. Strain through a jelly bag. Measure liquid. Measure 450 g (1 lb/2¼ cups) sugar for each 600 ml (1 pt ./2½ cups) juice.

Wash 2 (250 g/8 oz) jars in hot, soapy water; rinse. Keep hot until needed.

In a large saucepan, cook juice over low heat. Add sugar. Stir until sugar dissolves. Increase heat; boil rapidly until jelly reaches 105C (221F).

Remove from heat. Remove scum.

Ladle hot jelly into 1 hot jar at a time. Wipe rim of jar with a clean damp cloth. Cover. Fill and cover remaining jars.

Makes 2 (250 g/8 oz).

Blueberry and Apple Jelly

1.4 kg (3 lb.) blueberries, stems removed

1.4 kg (3 lb.) cooking apples, coarsely chopped

Juice of 2 lemons

Sugar

In a large saucepan, place blueberries and apples. Just cover with water, simmer until fruit is soft. Using a wooden spoon, crush blueberries to release juice. Strain through a jelly bag. Measure juice. Measure 450 g (1 lb/2¼ cups) sugar for each 600 ml (1 pt./2½ cups) juice.

Wash 3 (250 g/8 oz) jars in hot, soapy water; rinse. Keep hot until needed.

In a large saucepan, cook juice over low heat. Add lemon juice and sugar. Stir until sugar dissolves. Increase heat; boil rapidly until jelly reaches 221F (105C). Remove from heat. Remove scum.

Ladle hot jelly into 1 hot jar at a time. Wipe rim of jar with a clean damp cloth. Cover. Fill and cover remaining jars.

Makes 3 (250 g/8 oz).

Black Grape Jelly

1.4 kg (3 lb.) large sweet black grapes

Sugar

Remove grapes from stalks. In a large saucepan, simmer grapes until juice is released. Strain through a jelly bag. Measure juice. Measure 375 g (12 oz/1½ cups) sugar for each 600 ml (1 pt/2½ cups) juice.

Wash 2 (250 g/8 oz) jars in hot, soapy water; rinse. Keep hot until needed.

In a large saucepan, simmer juice 10 minutes. Add sugar. Stir until sugar dissolves. Increase heat; boil rapidly until jelly reaches 105C (221F). Remove from heat. Remove scum.

Ladle hot jelly into 1 hot jar at a time. Wipe rim of jar with a clean damp cloth. Cover. Fill and cover remaining jars.

Makes 2 (250 g/8 oz).

Blackcurrant Jelly

1.8 kg (4 lb.) blackcurrants, stems removed

1.7 l (3 pt/7½ cups) water

Sugar

In a large saucepan, simmer blackcurrants and water 1 hour or until blackcurrants are soft. Strain through a jelly bag. Measure juice. Measure 450 g (1 lb./2¼ cups) sugar for each 600 ml (1 pt/2½ cups) juice.

Wash 6 (250 g/8 oz) jars in hot, soapy water; rinse. Keep hot until needed.

In a large saucepan, cook juice over low heat. Add sugar. Stir until sugar dissolves. Increase heat; boil rapidly until jelly reaches 105C (221F). Remove from heat. Remove scum.

Ladle hot jelly into 1 hot jar at a time. Wipe rim of jar with a clean damp cloth. Cover. Fill and cover remaining jars.

Makes 6 (250 g/8 oz).

Herb Jelly

1.4 kg (3 lb.) cooking apples, coarsely chopped

1.4 l (2½ pt/6¼ cups) water

310 ml (10 fl oz/1¼ cups) white vinegar

Sugar

30 g (1 oz/½ cup) chopped fresh mint, tarragon, parsley or basil

Green food colouring

In a large saucepan, simmer apples, water and vinegar until apples are very soft. Strain through a jelly bag. Measure juice. Measure 450 g (1 lb./2¼ cups) sugar for each 600 ml (1 pt/2½ cups) juice.

Wash 2 (250 g/8 oz) jars in hot, soapy water; rinse. Keep hot until needed.

In a large saucepan, cook juice over low heat. Add sugar. Stir until sugar dissolves. Increase heat; boil rapidly 10-15, minutes or until jelly reaches 105C (221F). Remove from heat. Stir in mint, tarragon, parsley or basil. Tint with food colouring as desired. Remove scum.

Ladle hot jelly into 1 hot jar at a time. Wipe rim of jar with a clean damp cloth. Cover. Fill and cover remaining jars.

Makes 2 (250 g/8 oz).

Cranberry and Apple Jelly

1 kg (2 lb.) cranberries

1.4 kg (3 lb.) cooking apples, coarsely chopped

4 oranges, coarsely chopped

1.7 l (3 pt/7½ cups) water

Sugar

In a large saucepan, simmer cranberries, apples, oranges and water
1½ hours or until orange peel is soft. Strain through a jelly bag.
Measure juice. Measure 450 g (1 lb./2¼ cups) sugar for each 600 ml
(1 pt/2½ cups) juice.

Wash 3 (250 g/8 oz) jars in hot, soapy water; rinse. Keep hot until
needed.

In a large saucepan, cook juice over low heat. Add sugar. Stir until
sugar dissolves. Increase heat; boil rapidly until jelly reaches 105C
(221F). Remove from heat. Remove scum.

Ladle hot jelly into 1 hot jar at a time. Wipe rim of jar with a clean
damp cloth. Cover. Fill and cover remaining jars.

Makes 3 (250 g/8 oz).

MARMALADES

Marmalade is a sweetened jelly made from citrus fruit and peel. Pectin, which is essential for a good set, exists in the pith and pips of citrus fruits, so both are tied in a piece of muslin and boiled with the peel. Use as a spread on toast or bread or as flan filling.

Wash and dry citrus fruit. *For thick-skinned fruit*, remove peel and white pith. Shred peel; coarsely chop fruit. *For thin-skinned fruit*, thinly slice whole fruit in quarters lengthwise, cut fruit and peel together in thin or thick strips.

Tie white pith and pips into a piece of muslin. Place in a large saucepan.

Simmer fruit, all juices and water 1 to 1½ hours or until peel is very soft. To check if peel is done, test a cooled piece between finger and thumb for softness. Remove pip bag, squeezing liquid back into pan; discard.

Add sugar. Stir until sugar dissolves.

Increase heat. Boil rapidly until
marmalade reaches 105C (221F) or
when a small amount of marmalade
poured on a cool plate and left 1
minute wrinkles when pushed with a
finger.

Let stand 10 minutes. Stir well to
prevent peel rising. Ladle hot
marmalade into hot jars; cover.

Oxford Marmalade

1.4 kg (3 lb.) Seville oranges, halved, seeded

Juice of 1 lemon

2.8 l (5 pt/12½ cups) water

2.7 kg (6 lb./13½ cups) sugar

2 tablespoons black treacle

4 tablespoons whisky or rum, if desired

Squeeze juice from oranges. Tie pips in a muslin bag. Cut oranges in thick shreds. In a large saucepan, simmer orange and lemon juice, shredded oranges, muslin bag and water 2 hours or until orange peel is soft. Discard muslin bag. Add sugar and treacle. Stir until sugar dissolves. Increase heat; boil rapidly 15 to 20 minutes or until marmalade reaches 105C (221F).

Remove from heat. Let stand 10 minutes. Add whisky or rum, if desired.

Wash 12 (450 g/16 oz) jars in hot, soapy water; rinse. Keep hot until needed.

Stir well. Ladle hot marmalade into 1 hot jar at a time. Wipe rim of jar with a clean damp cloth. Cover. Fill and cover remaining jars.

Makes 12 (450 g/16 oz).

Pineapple and Orange Marmalade

3 oranges, thinly sliced crosswise, seeded

1 lemon, thinly sliced crosswise, seeded

2 (450 g/16 oz) cans crushed pineapple in syrup

1.8 kg (4 lb./9 cups) sugar

Quarter each citrus fruit slice. Tie pips in a muslin bag. In a large saucepan, just cover citrus fruit and muslin bag with water. Simmer 45 minutes or until peel is soft. Discard muslin bag. Add pineapple and syrup. Simmer 15 minutes. Add sugar. Stir until sugar dissolves. Increase heat; boil rapidly 20 to 25 minutes or until marmalade reaches 105C (221F).

Remove from heat. Let stand 10 minutes.

Wash 13 (250 g/8 oz) jars in hot, soapy water; rinse. Keep hot until needed.

Stir well. Ladle hot marmalade into 1 hot jar at a time. Wipe rim of jar with a clean damp cloth. Cover. Fill and cover remaining jars.

Makes 13 (250 g/8 oz).

Three Fruit Marmalade

2 grapefruit, quartered, peeled

2 oranges, quartered, peeled

4 lemons, quartered, peeled

3.4 l (6 pt/15 cups) water

2.7 kg (6 lb./13½ cups) sugar

Finely shred all citrus fruit peel. Remove thick white pith and membrane from grapefruit. Tie pips in a muslin bag. Coarsely chop all citrus fruit pulp.

In a large saucepan, simmer peel, muslin bag, pulp and water 1½ hours. Discard muslin bag. Add sugar. Stir until sugar dissolves. Increase heat; boil rapidly 15 to 20 minutes or until marmalade reaches 105C (221F).

Remove from heat. Let stand 10 minutes.

Wash 9 (450 g/16 oz) jars in hot, soapy water; rinse. Keep hot until needed.

Stir well. Ladle hot marmalade into 1 hot jar at a time. Wipe rim of jar with a clean damp cloth. Cover. Fill and cover remaining jars.

Makes 9 (450 g/16 oz).

Chunky Blender Marmalade

1 kg (2 lb.) Seville oranges, quartered

1 lemon, quartered, seeded

2.3 l (4 pt/10 cups) water

1.8 kg (4 lb./9 cups) sugar

Remove pips from fruit; tie in a muslin bag. In a food processor/
blender, process oranges and lemon with ½ of water until finely
chopped.

In large saucepan, boil fruit and liquid, muslin bag and remaining
water 1 hour. Reduce heat. Add sugar. Stir until sugar dissolves.
Increase heat; boil rapidly 15 to 20 minutes or until marmalade
reaches 105C (221F).

Remove from heat. Let stand 10 minutes.

Wash 13 (250 g/8 oz) jars in hot, soapy water; rinse. Keep hot until
needed.

Stir well. Ladle hot marmalade into 1 hot jar at a time. Wipe rim of
jars with a clean damp cloth. Cover. Fill and cover remaining jars.

Makes 13 (250 g/8 oz).

Lime Marmalade

12 limes

—

1.7 l (3 pt/7½ cups) water

—

1.4 kg (3 lb./6¾ cups) sugar

Peel limes thinly. Cut lime peel in very thin strips, squeeze the juice. Tie pips in a muslin bag. Coarsely chop lime pulp. In a large saucepan, simmer peel, pulp, juice, muslin bag and water 1¼ hours or until peel is very soft. Discard muslin bag. Add sugar. Stir until sugar dissolves. Increase heat; boil rapidly 10 to 15 minutes or until marmalade reaches 105C (221F).

Remove from heat. Let stand 10 minutes.

Wash 5 (450 g/16 oz) jars in hot, soapy water; rinse. Keep hot until needed.

Stir well. Ladle hot marmalade into 1 hot jar at a time. Wipe rim of jar with a clean damp cloth. Cover. Fill and cover remaining jars.

Makes 5 (450 g/16 oz).

— *Sweet Orange and Lemon Marmalade* —

4 oranges, thinly sliced crosswise, seeded

5 lemons, thinly sliced crosswise, seeded

2.8 l (5 pt./12½ cups) water

1.8 kg (4 lb./9 cups) sugar

Quarter each citrus fruit slice. Tie pips in a muslin bag. In a large saucepan, simmer citrus fruit and water 1½ hours. Discard muslin bag. Add sugar. Stir until sugar dissolves. Increase heat; boil rapidly 10 to 15 minutes or until marmalade reaches 105C (221F).

Remove from heat. Let stand 10 minutes.

Wash 13 (250 g/8 oz) jars in hot, soapy water; rinse. Keep hot until needed.

Stir well. Ladle hot marmalade into 1 hot jar at a time. Wipe rim of jar with a clean damp cloth. Cover. Fill and cover remaining jars.

Makes 13 (250 g/8 oz).

CURDS, BUTTERS & CHEESES

Curds are thick, creamy, fruit-flavoured mixtures of eggs, butter and sugar with a 1 to 2 month storage life. Butters and cheeses are thick mixtures of fruit pulp and sugar with a 6 month storage life. Serve as a spread on biscuits or bread, or use as a pie filling.

In a heatproof bowl combine sugar, butter and fruit juice.

Strain in whole eggs. Place top of a double saucepan or heatproof bowl over a pan of hot water.

Cook until mixture is thick and creamy. Stir constantly. Do not overcook. Ladle hot mixture into jars; cover.

Orange Curd with Candied Peel

Grated peel and juice of 4 large oranges

125 g (4 oz/½ cup) candied orange peel, chopped

220 g (7 oz/1 cup) sugar

250 g (8 oz/1 cup) unsalted butter

6 egg yolks, beaten

Wash 3 (250 g/8 oz) jars in hot, soapy water; rinse. Keep hot until needed. Prepare lids as manufacturer directs.

Strain orange juice. In top of a double saucepan or a heatproof bowl set over a pan of simmering water, cook orange peel and juice, candied peel, sugar and butter until butter melts and sugar dissolves. Stir often. Stir in egg yolks, a little at a time. Cook until thick and creamy. Stir constantly. Do not overcook.

Ladle hot curd into 1 hot jar at a time. Wipe rim of jar with a clean damp cloth. Fill and cover remaining jars.

Makes 3 (250 g/8 oz).

Spiced Apple Butter

1.4 kg (3 lb.) apples, coarsely chopped

600 ml (20 fl oz/2½ cups) water

600 ml (20 fl oz/2½ cups) cider

Light brown sugar

½ teaspoon ground cloves

½ teaspoon ground cinnamon

½ teaspoon ground nutmeg

In a large saucepan cook apples, water and cider over a low heat until apples are very soft. In a food processor/blender, process apples and liquid to a purée. Measure or weigh purée. Measure 350 g (12 oz/1¾ cups) sugar for each 450 g (1 lb./2 cups) purée. Set aside.

Wash 8 (250 g/8 oz) jars in hot, soapy water; rinse. Keep hot until needed.

In a large saucepan, cook purée over low heat 30 to 40 minutes until mixture resembles thick cream. Add spices and sugar. Stir until sugar dissolves. Simmer gently, stirring often, until liquid evaporates.

Ladle hot butter into 1 hot jar at a time. Wipe rim of jar with a clean damp cloth. Cover. Fill and cover remaining jars.

Makes 8 (250 g/8 oz).

Dried Apricot Cheese

450 g (1 lb./3 cups) dried apricots

1 orange

450 g (1 lb./2¼ cups) sugar

In a medium bowl, just cover apricots with water; let stand 12 hours.

In a large saucepan, cook apricots and liquid over medium heat until apricots are very soft. In a food processor/blender, process apricot and liquid to a purée. Set aside.

In a small saucepan, cover orange with water. Bring to a boil; cook until orange peel is very soft. Remove orange from pan; reserve liquid. Cool orange. Chop orange coarsely; discard pips. In a food processor/blender, process chopped orange and reserved liquid.

Wash 3 (250 g/8 oz) jars in hot, soapy water; rinse. Keep hot until needed.

In a large saucepan, cook apricot and orange purées and sugar over low heat. Stir until sugar dissolves. Increase heat; boil until mixture resembles thick cream.

Ladle hot butter into 1 hot jar at a time. Wipe rim of jar with a clean, damp cloth. Cover. Fill and cover remaining jars.

Makes 3 (250 g/8 oz).

Soft Fruit Butter

450 g (1 lb./4 cups) blackcurrants, stems removed

450 g (1 lb./4 cups) redcurrants, stems removed

450 g (1 lb./2¾ cups) gooseberries, cleaned

450 g (1 lb./3 cups) strawberries, hulled

900 g (2 lb./4½ cups) sugar

Wash 8 (250 g/8 oz) jars in hot, soapy water; rinse. Keep hot until needed.

In a large saucepan simmer all berries until juice runs from berries. Increase heat; cook 15 minutes. Reduce heat. Add sugar. Stir until sugar dissolves. Increase heat; boil rapidly 25 minutes or until very thick.

Ladle hot butter into 1 hot jar at a time. Wipe rim of jar with a clean damp cloth. Cover. Fill and cover remaining jars.

Makes 8 (250 g/8 oz).

Rich Lemon Curd

550 g (1¼ lb./2½ cups) sugar cubes

Juice of 4 large lemons, strained

185 g (6 oz/¾ cup) unsalted butter

7 eggs, beaten, strained

Wash 4 (250 g/8 oz) jars in hot, soapy water; rinse. Keep hot until needed.

Rub peel of lemons with sugar cubes. In a heat-proof bowl or top of double saucepan set over a pan of hot water, place sugar cubes, lemon juice, butter and eggs over low heat until thick and creamy; stir constantly. Do not overcook.

Ladle hot curd into 1 hot jar at a time. Wipe rim of jar with a clean damp cloth. Cover. Fill and cover remaining jars.

Makes 4 (250 g/8 oz).

CONSERVES

Conserves are thick sweetened mixtures
of fruit with such additions as
dried fruit, nuts and spirits or
liqueurs. Conserves may
be served with cream, as
a sauce for ice-cream,
used as flan fillings
or as a spread.

Prepare fruit according to recipe. In a
large saucepan simmer fruit, sugar
and water until fruit is soft.

Cook until thick. Conserves are more
syrupy than jams and do not set. Stir
in dried fruits, nuts and alcohol as
directed.

Ladle hot conserve into hot jars;
cover.

Pineapple Harlequin

1 (250 g./8 oz.) can crushed pineapple in syrup

450 g (1 lb./2 cups) dark sweet cherries

450 g (1 lb./4 cups) redcurrants, stems removed

2 oranges, thinly sliced, pips removed, cored

450 g (1 lb./3 cups) raspberries, stems removed

Sugar

Drain pineapple; reserve syrup. Measure or weigh fruit. Mix . Measure 450 g (1 lb./ 2 cups) sugar for each 450 g (1 lb.) fruit. Set aside.

In a large saucepan, cook fruit and reserved pineapple syrup. Add reserved sugar. Stir until sugar dissolves. Increase heat; boil rapidly 15 minutes until mixture thickens.

Wash 8 (250 g/8 oz) jars in hot, soapy water; rinse. Keep hot until needed,
Ladle hot mixture into 1 hot jar at a time. Wipe rim of jar with a clean damp cloth. Cover. Fill and cover remaining jars.

Makes 8 (250 g/8 oz).

Lemon Apples in Wine

Peel and juice of 8 lemons

600 ml (1 pt/2½ cups) boiling water

600 ml (1 pt/2½ cups) dry white wine

2 kg (4½ lb./9 cups) sugar

2.3½ kg (5 lb.) eating apples, peeled, cored, sliced thinly

2 tablespoons brandy

In a large bowl, cover lemon peel with boiling water and wine. Let stand 30 minutes.

Wash 13 (250 g/8 oz) jars in hot, soapy water; rinse. Keep hot until needed.

In a large saucepan, cook peel and liquid, lemon juice and sugar over low heat. Stir until sugar dissolves. Increase heat; boil 10 minutes. Remove from heat. Strain liquid; return liquid to pan. Discard peel. Add apples. Cook over low heat until apples are soft and liquid resembles thin cream. Remove from heat. Stir in brandy.

Ladle hot mixture into 1 hot jar at a time. Wipe rim of jar with a clean damp cloth. Cover. Fill and cover remaining jars.

Makes 13 (250 g/8 oz).

Orange Walnut Conserve

1 kg (2 lb.) oranges

1.7 l (3 pt/7½ cups) water

125 g (4 oz/⅔ cup) raisins

900 g (2 lb./4½ cups) sugar

60 g (2 oz/½ cup) walnuts, coarsely chopped

Finely grate orange peel; set aside. Remove remaining pith; discard. Chop flesh; discard pips.

In a large saucepan cook orange flesh and water over low heat 30 minutes. Remove from heat. Measure 1.1 l (2 pt/5 cups) pulp. Add water if necessary to make correct measure.

Wash 6 (250g /8 oz) jars in hot, soapy water; rinse. Keep hot until needed.

In a large saucepan, cook pulp, reserved peel, raisins and sugar, over low heat. Stir until sugar dissolves. Increase heat; boil rapidly 20 minutes. Stir in walnuts; bring to a boil again.

Ladle hot conserve into 1 hot jar at a time. Wipe rim of jar with a clean damp cloth. Cover. Fill and cover remaining jars.

Makes 6 (250 g/8 oz).

Plum, Rum and Raisin Conserve

1.8 kg (4 lb.) plums, halved

185 g (6 oz/1 cup) raisins

310 ml (10 fl oz/1¼ cups) water, if needed

1.1kg (1½ lb./6 cups) sugar

125 g (4 oz/1 cup) blanched almonds, chopped

4 tablespoons dark rum

Wash 10 (250 g/8 oz) jars in hot, soapy water; rinse. Keep hot until needed.

In a large saucepan, simmer plums and raisins until plums are very soft. If plums are not juicy, add water.

Add sugar. Stir until sugar dissolves. Increase heat; boil rapidly until thickened. Remove from heat. Stir in almonds and rum.

Ladle hot conserve into 1 hot jar at a time. Wipe rim of jar with a clean damp cloth. Cover. Fill and cover remaining jars.

Makes 10 (250 g/8 oz).

Pear and Pineapple Conserve

1 kg (2 lb.) pears, peeled, cored, thinly sliced

250 ml (8 fl oz/1 cup) water

450 g (1 lb./2¼ cups) sugar

1 small pineapple, peeled, coarsely grated

Wash 5 (250 g/8 oz) jars in hot, soapy water; rinse. Keep hot until needed. Prepare lids as manufacturer directs.

In a large saucepan, bring pears, water and sugar to a boil over low heat. Add pineapple. Simmer 45 minutes.

Ladle hot conserve into 1 hot jar at a time. Wipe rim of jar with a clean damp cloth. Cover. Fill and cover remaining jars.

Makes 5 (250 g/8 oz).

FREEZER JAMS

Freezer jam has a fresher, more natural fruit taste and a brighter colour than cooked jam. Both contain fruit or fruit juices, pectin and sugar. Fresh or frozen fruit can be used including strawberries, nectarines, peaches and apricots. Serve freezer jam as a spread on bread, toast or muffins, or as a tart filling.

Measure fresh or thawed frozen fruit exactly. In a large bowl, place fruit and sugar. Mash slightly. Let stand 20 minutes. Stir occasionally.

Add liquid pectin; stir 3 minutes.

Ladle jam into clean freezer containers; cover and label. Let stand 5 hours.

Refrigerate 24 to 48 hours or until jam
sets.

Store in freezer up to 6 months.

To serve, let stand 1 hour at room
temperature. Refrigerate leftover
jam. Use within 2 days.

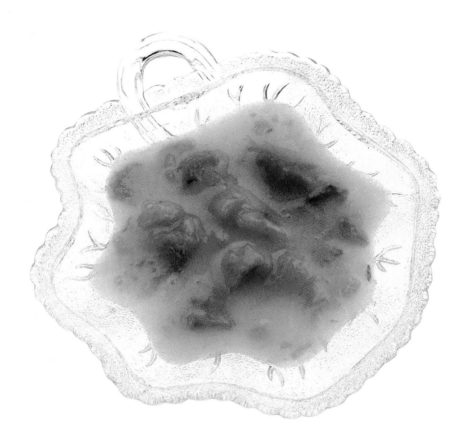

Freezer Nectarine Jam

750 g (1½ lb.) ripe nectarines, peeled, stones removed, coarsely chopped

900 g (2 lb./4½ cups) caster sugar

125 ml (4 fl oz/½ cup) liquid pectin

1 teaspoon citric acid

Wash 6 (250 g/8 oz) freezer containers and lids in hot, soapy water; rinse.

In a large bowl, mash nectarines well. Add sugar and citric acid. Let stand 20 minutes. Stir occasionally. Add liquid pectin; stir 3 minutes.

Ladle jam into prepared containers. Wipe rim of container with a clean damp cloth. Cover. Let stand 5 hours.

Refrigerate 24 to 48 hours or until jam jells.

Store in freezer up to 6 months. To serve, let stand 1 hour at room temperature. Refrigerate leftover jam up to 2 days.

VARIATION:Fresh ripe peaches or apricots may also be used for this recipe.

Makes 6 (250 g/8 oz).

Freezer Strawberry Jam

750 g (1½ lb./5 cups) strawberries, hulled, quartered

900 g (2 lb./4½ cups) caster sugar

125 ml (4 fl oz/½ cup) liquid pectin

Wash 6 (250 g/8 oz) freezer containers and lids in hot, soapy water; rinse.

In a large bowl, mash strawberries lightly using a fork. Add sugar. Let stand 20 minutes. Stir occasionally. Add liquid pectin; stir 3 minutes.

Ladle jam into prepared containers. Wipe rim of container with a clean damp cloth. Cover. Let stand 5 hours.

Refrigerate 24 to 48 hours or until jam jells.

Store in freezer up to 6 months. To serve, let stand 1 hour at room temperature. Refrigerate leftover jam up to 2 days.

Makes 6 (250 g/8 oz).

MICROWAVE PRESERVES

Preserves and condiments can be made very successfully in a microwave oven, saving time and energy. The method is different to standard jam and chutney making, so follow the instructions carefully.

If fruit, such as raspberries, is frozen, defrost on low power 3 to 4 minutes or until soft.

Use a large microwave-safe bowl, twice volume of ingredients.

Add water, if necessary. Lightly cover. Microwave on full power for time specified in recipe.

Stir in sugar. Microwave uncovered on full power for specified time, stirring occasionally.

Test for setting, page 12.

Stir well. Cool 5 minutes. Stir again. Pour into hot jars; cover.

Microwave Raspberry Jam

450 g (1 lb./3 cups) raspberries

2 tablespoons lemon juice

450 g (1 lb./2¼ cups) sugar

Wash 3 (250 g/8 oz) jars in hot, soapy water; rinse. Keep hot until needed.

In a large microwave-safe bowl, microwave raspberries, lemon juice and sugar on full power 5 minutes, stirring occasionally until sugar dissolves. Microwave on full power 12 minutes or until jam reaches 105C (221F). Let stand 5 minutes.

Stir well. Ladle hot jam into 1 hot jar at a time. Wipe rim of jar with a clean damp cloth. Cover. Fill and cover remaining jars.

Makes 3 (250 g/8 oz).

Microwave Lemon Curd

125 g (4 oz/½ cup) butter or margarine

Grated peel and juice of 3 large lemons

250 g (8 oz/1 cup) sugar

3 eggs, beaten

1 egg yolk, beaten

Wash 2 (250 g/8 oz) jars in hot, soapy water; rinse. Keep hot until needed.

In a large microwave-safe bowl, microwave butter and lemon peel and juice on full power 3 minutes. Stir in sugar. Microwave 2 minutes. Stir in eggs and egg yolk, a little at a time. Microwave on low power 12 to 15 minutes or until curd thickens, stirring occasionally.

Ladle hot curd into 1 hot jar at a time. Wipe rim of jar with a clean damp cloth. Cover. Fill and cover remaining jars.

Makes 2 (250 g/8 oz).

Microwave Spiced Oranges

5 Valencia oranges, sliced thinly crosswise

310 ml (10 fl oz/1¼ cups) water

310 ml (10 fl oz/1¼ cups) white wine vinegar

375 g (12 oz/1¾ cups) sugar

1 (5-cm/2-in) cinnamon stick

6 to 10 whole cloves

In a large microwave-safe bowl, microwave oranges and water, tightly covered, on full power 15 to 20 minutes or until orange peel is very soft, strain; discard water.

In a medium microwave-safe bowl, microwave vinegar, sugar and cinnamon on full power 10 minutes, stirring occasionally until sugar dissolves.

Add orange slices. Microwave, tightly covered, on low power 25 to 30 minutes or until orange peel is transparent.

Wash 2 (250 g/8 oz) jars in hot, soapy water; rinse. Keep hot until needed.

Place 3 to 5 cloves in each hot jar. Using a slotted spoon, pack orange slices into hot jars.

Microwave remaining syrup on full power 7 minutes. Strain syrup. Ladle hot syrup over orange slices. Wipe rim of jars with a clean damp cloth. Cover with vinegar-proof lids.

Makes 2 (250 g/8 oz).

Microwave Cucumber Relish

2 large cucumbers, chopped

2 medium onions, finely chopped

2 tablespoons cooking salt

310 ml (10 fl oz/1¼ cups) white vinegar

90 g (3 oz/½ cup) sugar

½ teaspoon celery seeds

½ teaspoon mustard seeds

In a medium bowl, combine cucumber, onions and salt. Let stand 2 hours. Rinse under cold running water; drain. Set aside.

Wash 2 (250 g/8 oz) jars in hot, soapy water; rinse. Keep hot until needed.

In a large microwave-safe bowl, microwave vinegar, sugar and celery and mustard seeds on full power 6 minutes, stirring 2 to 3 times. Stir in cucumber mixture. Microwave on full power 2 minutes.

Ladle hot relish into 1 hot jar at a time. Wipe rim of jar with a clean damp cloth. Cover. Fill and cover remaining jars.

Let mature 1 month before using.

Makes 2 (250 g/8 oz).

PICKLES

Pickled fruits and vegetables and relishes are products with crisp, sour or sweet-sour flavour. Good quality vinegar is essential for pickling. Choose a vinegar containing at least 5% acetic acid or it will not preserve fruit or vegetables. Use pickles and relishes as an accompaniment with meats or with curries or spicy foods.

Use fruit and vegetables of high quality. Avoid soft fruit and vegetables. Prepare by chopping or slicing according to recipe.

If specified in recipe, soak vegetables in brine using 250 g (8 oz/2 cups) salt to 2 l (3½ pt/7 cups) water, or 90 g (3 oz/¾ cup) salt to 750 g (1½ lb.) vegetables. Let stand 24 hours to withdraw some natural juices which dilute preserving vinegar.

Drain. Rinse under cold running water. Drain thoroughly. If using fruit, cook in liquid as directed.

Prepare spiced or sweetened vinegar.

Add fruit or vegetables to vinegar and cook for specified time.

Pack hot fruit or vegetables and vinegar mixture into hot jars; cover with vinegar-proof lids.

Spiced Prunes

450 g (1 lb./3 cups) large prunes

450 ml (16 fl oz/2 cups) cold steeped tea

600 ml (1 pt/2½ cups) white wine vinegar

450 g (1 lb./2¼ cups) sugar

1 2.5-cm (1in.) cinnamon stick

1 teaspoon cloves

10 allspice berries

Blade of mace

In a large bowl, cover prunes with tea. Let stand 12 hours.
   Wash 2 (450 g/16 oz) jars in hot, soapy water; rinse. Keep hot until needed.
   In a large saucepan, cook prunes and liquid over low heat 15 to 20 minutes until prunes are plump.
   In a large saucepan, bring vinegar, sugar and spices to a boil. Reduce heat; simmer 5 minutes. Add prunes and liquid. Simmer 5 minutes. Using a slotted spoon, pack hot prunes into hot jars.
   Increase heat; bring syrup to a boil. Ladle hot syrup over prunes. Wipe rim of jars with a clean damp cloth. Cover.
   Let mature 1 week before using.

Makes 2 (450 g/16 oz).

Pickled Aubergines

1.8 kg (4 lb.) aubergines, peeled, cut in julienne pieces

4 tablespoons salt

1 l (1¾pt /4½ cups) white wine vinegar

2 tablespoons sugar

125 ml (4 fl oz/½ cup) olive oil

3 tablespoon chopped fresh chives

2 tablespoons chopped fresh marjoram or oregano

2 dried chilli peppers

8 garlic cloves, halved

Wash 4 (450 g/16 oz) jars in hot, soapy water; rinse. Keep hot until needed.

Place aubergines in a colander. Sprinkle with salt. Shake colander. Drain 30 minutes. In a large saucepan bring vinegar and sugar to a boil. Add aubergines. Bring to a boil. Reduce heat; simmer 5 minutes. Drain. Reserve liquid.

Mix hot aubergines, olive oil, chives and marjoram or oregano. Pack into hot jars. Add 1 chilli pepper and 4 garlic pieces to each jar. Using a wooden spoon, press aubergines to release juice. Ladle reserved liquid over aubergines. Wipe rim of jars with a clean damp cloth. Cover.

Let mature 1 month before using.

Makes 4 (450 g/16 oz).

Chow Chow

450 g (1 lb.) cucumbers, peeled, diced

450 g (1 lb.) onions, chopped

450 g (1 lb.) green tomatoes, chopped

450 g (1 lb.) green beans, chopped

450 g (1 lb.) celery, finely chopped

450 g (1 lb.) small cauliflower florets

450 g (1 lb.) hard white cabbage, shredded

4 tablespoons cooking salt

1.1 l (2 pt/5 cups) malt vinegar

250 g (8 oz/1 cup) sugar

5 tablespoons dry mustard

3 tablespoons plain flour

1 tablespoon turmeric

In a large bowl, combine all vegetables. Sprinkle with salt. Cover with cold water. Let stand 24 hours. Drain. Add ½ of vinegar. Let stand 12 hours.

In a small bowl, mix sugar, mustard, flour, turmeric and a small amount of remaining vinegar. In a large saucepan, bring remaining vinegar to a boil. Stir in mustard mixture. Reduce heat; simmer 2 minutes. Add vegetables and liquid. Increase heat; bring to a boil. Simmer 20 minutes, stirring often.

Wash 6 (450 g/ 16 oz) jars in hot, soapy water; rinse. Keep hot until needed.

Pack hot Chow Chow into 1 hot jar at a time. Wipe rim of jar with a clean damp cloth. Cover. Fill and cover remaining jars.

Let mature 1 month before using.

Makes 6 (450 g/16 oz).

Demerara Pickled Peaches

1 kg (2 lb.) small firm peaches, peeled

310 ml (10 fl oz/1¼ cups) white wine vinegar

450 g (1 lb./2¼ cups) demerara sugar

1 (2.5-cm/1-in.) cinnamon stick

6 whole cloves

Wash 5 (250 g/8 oz) jars in hot, soapy water; rinse. Keep hot until needed.

In a large saucepan, cook vinegar, sugar and spices over low heat. Stir until sugar dissolves. Add peaches. Increase heat; bring to a boil. Reduce heat; simmer until peaches are soft but not broken.

Using a slotted spoon, pack hot peaches in hot jars.

Increase heat; bring syrup to a boil. Ladle hot syrup over peaches. Wipe rim of jars with a clean damp cloth. Cover.

Makes 5 (250 g/8 oz).

Italian Fruit Mustard Pickles

850 g (1¾ lb./3¾ cups) sugar

250 ml (8 fl oz/1 cup) water

1 kg (2 lb.) mixed fruit, (peaches, apricots, plums, cherries, figs and melons), peeled, pitted, chopped

150 ml (5 fl oz/⅔ cup) white wine vinegar

4 tablespoons mustard powder

In a large saucepan, cook 750 g (1½ lb./3 cups) sugar and water over low heat 15 minutes or until sugar dissolves. Add fruit. Simmer 15 minutes or until fruit is soft but not broken. Remove from heat; cool.

In a small saucepan, cook remaining sugar and vinegar over low heat 15 minutes. Remove from heat; cool. Mix in mustard. Let stand 1 hour.

Wash 5 (250 g/8 oz) jars in hot, soapy water; rinse. Keep hot until needed.

Stir mustard syrup into fruit. Pack hot fruit into hot jars. Ladle hot syrup over fruit. Wipe rim of jars with a clean damp cloth. Cover.

Let mature 24 hours. Store up to 6 months.

Makes 5 (250 g/8 oz).

Pickled Dill Cucumbers

3.5 kg (7 lb.) pickling cucumbers, about 8-cm (3-in) long

1 l (35 fl oz/4½ cups) cider vinegar

1.6 kg (3½ lb./8 cups) sugar

2 tablespoons cooking salt

2 tablespoons mixed pickling spice

2 tablespoons dill seed

In a large bowl, cover cucumber with boiling water. Let stand 24 hours. Drain. Repeat process 3 days. Use fresh water each time.

In a large saucepan, bring vinegar, sugar, salt and pickling spice to a boil. Pour over cucumbers. Let stand 24 hours. Drain. Reserve liquid.

Wash 10 (450 g/16 oz) jars in hot, soapy water; rinse. Keep hot until needed.

In a large saucepan, bring reserved liquid to a boil. Add cucumber. Bring to a boil. Pack hot cucumbers into hot jars. Divide dill seed between jars. Bring liquid again to a boil. Ladle hot liquid over cucumbers. Wipe rim of jars with a clean damp cloth. Cover.

Let mature 2 weeks before using.

Makes 10 (450 g/16 oz).

Pickled Pears

900 g (2 lb./4 cups) sugar

600 ml (1 pt/2½ cups) white wine vinegar

1½ tablespoons whole cloves

1½ tablespoons whole allspice

Large piece of dried ginger root, mashed

1 (8-cm/3-in) cinnamon stick

Grated peel of ½ lemon

1.8 kg (4 lb.) small pears, peeled, cored, quartered

In a large saucepan, cook sugar and vinegar over low heat. Stir until sugar dissolves . Tie cloves, allspice, ginger root, cinnamon stick and lemon peel in a piece of muslin. Suspend in pan so spices are immersed in liquid. Add pears. Simmer 40 minutes or until pears are soft but not broken.

Wash 4 (450 g/16 oz) jars in hot, soapy water; rinse. Keep hot until needed.

Using a slotted spoon, pack hot pears in hot jars. Discard muslin bag. Increase heat; boil syrup 10 minutes or until syrupy. Ladle hot syrup over pears. Wipe rim of jars with a clean damp cloth. Cover.

Let mature 1 month before using.

Makes 4 (450 g/16 oz).

Pickled Lemons

12 lemons

2 tablespoons cooking salt

850 ml (1½ pt / 3¾ cups) white wine vinegar

12 white peppercorns

Large piece of dried ginger root, mashed

3 tablespoons white mustard seeds

2 garlic cloves, crushed

Using a sharp knife, cut skins of lemons lengthwise without cutting flesh. Rub salt into cuts. In a shallow bowl, let lemons stand 5 days in a cool place. Turn lemons occasionally. Drain, reserve liquid. In a large saucepan, bring reserved liquid, vinegar, peppercorns and ginger to a boil. Reduce heat; simmer 5 minutes. Add lemons. Simmer 30 minutes.

Wash 5 (250 g/8 oz) jars in hot, soapy water; rinse. Keep hot until needed.

Using a slotted spoon, pack hot lemons in hot jars. Add mustard seeds and garlic to liquid. Increase heat; bring to a boil. Remove ginger. Remove scum. Ladle hot liquid over lemons. Wipe rim of jars with a clean damp cloth. Cover.

Makes 5 (250 g/8 oz).

CHUTNEYS

Chutney is a condiment that is made of fruits or vegetables cooked in vinegar, sweetened with sugar or dried fruit and flavoured with spices. Chutneys should be smooth and pulpy with a mellow flavour and are best left to mature to blend flavours for at least 1 month. Use as an accompaniment to meats, curries, cheese, and savoury pies or as a filling for sandwiches.

Prepare fruit and vegetables according to recipe. Remove all bruises. Chop finely, mince, or process in a food processor/blender.

In a large saucepan cook fruit, dried fruit, vegetables and vinegar over low heat to soften ingredients and break down fibres.

Add remaining vinegar, sugar and spices.

Cook over low heat, stirring often, 1
hour or until chutney is thick and
golden brown with no excess liquid.

Remove from heat. Stir well. Ladle or
pour hot chutney into hot jars; cover
with vinegar-proof lids.

Let mature to blend flavours 1 month
before using.

Mixed Fruit Chutney

450 g (1 lb.) plums, halved, stoned. roughly chopped

1 kg (2 lb.) tomatoes, peeled, coarsely chopped

1.8 kg (4 lb.) cooking apples, peeled, cored, finely chopped

1 kg (2 lb.) ripe pears, peeled, cored, finely chopped

1.8 kg (4 lb./10⅔ cups) dark brown sugar

450 g (1 lb./2½ cups) seedless raisins

1.2 l (2pt/5 cups) malt vinegar

1½ tablespoons salt

1 teaspoon ground black pepper

1 teaspoon ground ginger

1 teaspoon ground cloves

1 teaspoon ground mace

1 teaspoon cayenne pepper

In a large saucepan, mix plums, tomatoes, apples and pears. Stir in sugar, raisins, vinegar, salt and spices. Bring to a boil, stirring well. Reduce heat; simmer 1¼ hours or until thick and golden brown. Stir often.

Wash 10 (450 g/16 oz) jars in hot, soapy water; rinse. Keep hot until needed.

Ladle hot chutney into 1 hot jar at a time. Wipe rim of jar with clean damp cloth. Cover. Fill and cover remaining jars.

Let mature 1 month before using.

Makes 10 (450 g/16 oz).

Apple Ginger Chutney

1.4 kg (3 lb.) cooking apples, peeled, cored, finely chopped

375 g (12 oz/2 cups) light brown sugar

600 ml (1 pt/2½ cups) cider vinegar

1½ tablespoons salt

1½ teaspoons ground ginger

1 teaspoon ground allspice

1 teaspoon ground cloves

1 green pepper, finely chopped

1 medium onion, finely chopped

125 g (4 oz/½ cup) preserved ginger in syrup, finely chopped

125 g (4 oz/⅔ cup) sultanas

Grated peel and juice of ½ lemon

In a large saucepan, bring apples, sugar, vinegar, salt and spices to a boil, stirring well. Reduce heat; simmer 10 minutes. Add pepper, onion, ginger and syrup, sultanas and lemon peel and juice. Increase heat; bring to a boil. Reduce heat; simmer 1 hour or until thick and golden brown. Stir often.

Wash 3 (450 g/16 oz) jars in hot, soapy water; rinse. Keep hot until needed.

Ladle hot chutney into 1 hot jar at a time. Wipe rim of jar with a clean damp cloth. Cover. Fill and cover remaining jars.

Let mature 1 month before using.

Makes 3 (450 g/16 oz).

Sweet Grape Chutney

1 kg (2 lb.) white grapes, halved, seeded

1 kg (2 lb.) cooking apples, peeled, cored, finely chopped

550 g (1¼ lb/3⅓ cups) light soft brown sugar

250 g (8 oz/1¼ cup) sultanas

310 ml (10 fl oz/1¼ cups) cider vinegar

155 ml (5 fl oz/⅔ cup) lemon juice

Grated peel of ½ lemon

½ teaspoon ground allspice

½ teaspoon ground cloves

½ teaspoon salt

¼ teaspoon ground cinnamon

Pinch of paprika

In a large saucepan, bring all ingredients to a boil, stirring well. Reduce heat; simmer 1 hour or until thick and golden brown. Stir often.

Wash 3 (450 g/16 oz) jars in hot, soapy water; rinse. Keep hot until needed.

Ladle hot chutney into 1 hot jar at a time. Wipe rim of jar with a clean damp cloth. Cover. Fill and cover remaining jars.

Let mature 1 month before using.

Makes 3 (450 g/16 oz).

Lemon Chutney

6 large lemons, thinly sliced crosswise, seeded

250 g (½ lb.) onions, finely chopped

1½ tablespoons cooking salt

Water

450 ml (16 fl oz/2 cups) cider vinegar

250 g (8 oz/1⅓ cups) light brown sugar

125 g (4 oz/½ cup) sultanas

1½ tablespoons white mustard seeds

1 teaspoon ground ginger

½ teaspoon cayenne pepper

In a large bowl, mix lemon slices and onions. Sprinkle with salt. Let stand 24 hours.

Wash 3 (250 g/8 oz) jars in hot, soapy water; rinse. Keep hot until needed.

In a large saucepan, place lemons, onions and liquid. Just cover with water, cook over low heat until lemon peel is soft but not broken. Add vinegar, sugar, sultanas and spices. Increase heat; bring to a boil, stirring well. Reduce heat; simmer 1 hour or until thick and golden brown. Stir often.

Ladle hot chutney into 1 hot jar at a time. Wipe rim of jar with a clean damp cloth. Cover. Fill and cover remaining jars.

Let mature 1 month before using.

Makes 3 (250 g/8 oz).

Banana Chutney

8 large ripe bananas, peeled, thinly sliced

450 g (1 lb.) onions, finely chopped

250 g (8 oz/1¼ cups) dates, stoned, chopped

125 g (4 oz/⅔ cup) crystallized ginger, chopped

600 ml (1 pt/2½ cups) cider vinegar

250 g (8 oz/1⅓ cups) light brown sugar

1 tablespoon salt

1 tablespoon mixed pickling spice

Wash 2 (450 g/16 oz) jars in hot, soapy water; rinse. Keep hot until needed.

In a large saucepan, mix bananas, onions, dates, ginger, vinegar, sugar and salt. Tie pickling spice in a 15-cm (6-in) square of muslin. Suspend in pan so spices are immersed in liquid. Bring to a boil. Reduce heat; simmer 1 hour or until thick and golden brown. Stir often.

Remove muslin bag. Ladle hot chutney into 1 hot jar at a time. Wipe rim of jar with a clean damp cloth. Cover. Fill and cover remaining jars.

Let mature at least 1 month before using.

Makes 2 (450 g/16 oz).

Mango Chutney

6 ripe mangoes, peeled, thinly sliced

310 ml (10 fl oz/1¼ cups) cider vinegar

250 g (8 oz/1⅓ cups) light brown sugar

45 g (1½ oz.) fresh ginger root, peeled, chopped

2 garlic cloves, crushed

2 teaspoons chilli powder

1 teaspoon salt

In a large saucepan, cook mangoes and vinegar over low heat 10 minutes. Stir in sugar, ginger, garlic, chilli powder and salt. Increase heat; bring slowly to a boil, stirring well. Reduce heat; simmer 30 minutes. Stir occasionally.

Wash 1 (250 g/8 oz) jar in hot, soapy water; rinse. Keep hot until needed.

Ladle hot chutney into 1 hot jar at a time. Wipe rim of jar with a clean damp cloth. Cover. Fill and cover remaining jars.

Let mature 1 month before using.

Makes 1 (250 g/8 oz).

Mint Chutney

2.5 kg (5 lb.) cooking apples, peeled, cored, finely chopped

450 g (1 lb./2⅔ cups) demerara sugar

600 ml (20 floz/2½ cups) cider vinegar

250 g (8 oz/2 cups) onions, chopped

250 g (8 oz/1¼ cups) stoned dates, chopped

250 g (8 oz/1¼ cup) sultanas

1 tablespoon salt

1 tablespoon ground ginger

4 tablespoons fresh mint, finely chopped

In a large saucepan, bring all ingredients except mint to a boil, stirring well. Reduce heat; simmer 1¼ hours or until thick and golden brown. Stir often. Stir in mint.

Wash 6 (450 g/16 oz) jars in hot water; rinse. Keep hot until needed.

Ladle hot chutney into 1 hot jar at a time. Wipe rim of jar with a clean damp cloth. Cover. Fill and cover remaining jars.

Let mature 1 month before using.

Makes 6 (450 g/16 oz).

Apricot Chutney

1 kg (2 lb.) apricots, peeled, pitted, chopped

450 g (1 lb.) onions, finely chopped

450 g (1 lb./2⅔ cups) dark brown sugar

600 ml (1 pt/2½ cups) white wine vinegar

250 g (8 oz/1¼ cup) preserved ginger, chopped

Grated peel and juice of 1 orange

1½ tablespoons salt

2 teaspoons white mustard seeds

1 teaspoon cayenne pepper

½ teaspoon ground turmeric

125 g (4 oz/1 cup) walnut halves

In a large saucepan, mix apricots, onions, sugar and vinegar. Stir in ginger, orange peel and juice, salt and spices. Bring to a boil. Reduce heat; simmer 1 hour until thick and golden brown. Stir often.

Wash 3 (450 g/16 oz) jars in hot, soapy water; rinse. Keep hot until needed.

Stir walnut halves into chutney. Ladle hot chutney into 1 hot jar at a time. Wipe rim of jar with a clean damp cloth. Cover. Fill and cover remaining jars.

Let mature 1 month before using.

Makes 3 (450 g/16 oz).

SAUCES & KETCHUPS

Sauces and ketchups are condiments or relishes for food. Serve as an accompaniment to meats, poultry or savoury pies or use in the preparation of savoury dishes.

Prepare fruit and/or vegetables according to recipe.

In a large saucepan, cook vinegar, sugar and flavouring ingredients over low heat until fruit and vegetables are very soft.

Strain through a sieve. Press through as much purée as possible.

Cook over low heat, stirring
frequently, until mixture is thick and
smooth.

Pour into hot sterilized bottles, cover
with vinegar-proof lids.

Release lids a half turn and place
bottles in a large pan or water bath on a
rack. When all bottles are in place,
pour hot water around bottles to
cover. Bring water slowly to a
temperature of 54C (150F). Simmer 30
minutes. Remove bottles; tighten lids
immediately. Cool; store.

Mixed Fruit Sauce

1.4 kg (3 lb.) red or green tomatoes, coarsely chopped

1.4 kg (3 lb.) cooking apples, peeled, cored, chopped

450 g (1 lb.) onions, chopped

750 g (1½ lb./4 cups) raisins

250 g (8 oz/1½ cups) stoned dates, chopped

850 ml (1½ pt/3¾ cups) white vinegar

2 teaspoons salt

1 teaspoon ground mixed spice, ginger and mustard powder

½ teaspoon ground cloves and cayenne pepper

Pinch of ground mace and chilli powder

750 g (1½ lb./4 cups) light brown sugar

In a large saucepan, bring tomatoes, apples, onions, raisins, dates, vinegar, salt and spices to a boil. Reduce heat; simmer 1 hour or until fruit and vegetables are soft. Strain through a sieve. In a large saucepan, cook purée and sugar over low heat. Stir until sugar dissolves. Increase heat; bring to a boil. Reduce heat; simmer 45 minutes or until thick.

Wash 8 (250 g/8 oz) jars in hot, soapy water; rinse. Keep hot until needed.

Ladle hot sauce into 1 hot jar at a time. Wipe rim of jar with a clean damp cloth. Cover. Fill and cover remaining jars. Sterilize 30 minutes in a water bath, page 93.

Makes 8 (250 g/8 oz).

Walnut Ketchup

80 green walnuts, casings split

1.8 (3 pt./7½ cups) vinegar

250 g (8 oz) onions, chopped

185 g (6 oz/1½ cups) non-iodized salt

1 tablespoon black peppercorns

1 tablespoon allspice berries

12 whole cloves

6 blades of mace

Use walnuts before shells form inside green casing. In a food processor/blender, chop walnuts. In a large saucepan, bring vinegar, onions, salt and spices to a boil.

In a large bowl, cover chopped walnuts with boiling liquid. Cover; let stand 14 days in a cold place. Stir each day. Strain through a jelly bag. In a large saucepan, bring strained liquid to a boil. Simmer 1 hour.

Wash 5 (250 g/8 oz) jars in hot, soapy water; rinse. Keep hot until needed.

Ladle hot vinegar into 1 hot jar at a time. Wipe rim of jar with clean damp cloth. Cover. Fill and cover remaining jars. Sterilize 30 minutes in a water bath, page 93.

Add to soups, stews and casseroles.

Makes 5 (250 g/8 oz).

Mushroom Ketchup

1 kg (2 lb.) large, dark, open mushrooms

90 g (3 oz/¾ cup) cooking salt

600 ml (1 pt/2½ cups) vinegar

1 (5-cm/2 inch) piece of dried ginger root

6 blades of mace

4 whole cloves

1 teaspoon allspice

1 teaspoon black peppercorns

1 (2.5-cm/1-in.) cinnamon stick

Cut off bottom of mushroom stalks; discard. Break mushrooms and stalks into small pieces. In a large ovenware bowl layer mushrooms and salt. Cover. Let stand in cool place 5 days. Stirring each day.

Preheat oven to 150C (300F). Cover mushrooms and liquid with foil. Place in oven 1½ hours. Strain through a jelly bag. In a large saucepan, bring liquid, vinegar, ginger and spices to a boil. Reduce heat; simmer until liquid is reduced ½. Strain through a jelly bag. In a large saucepan bring liquid to a boil.

Wash 2 (250 g/8 oz) jars in hot, soapy water; rinse. Keep hot until needed.

Ladle hot vinegar into 1 hot jar at a time, leaving ½-cm (¼-in.) headspace. Wipe rim of jar with a clean damp cloth. Cover. Fill and cover remaining jars. Sterilize 30 minutes in a water bath, page 93.

Makes 2 (250 g/8 oz).

Spiced Cranberry Sauce

1.8 kg (4 lb.) cranberries

450 g (1 lb.) onions finely chopped

450 g (1 lb/2¼ cups) sugar

450 ml (16 fl oz/2 cups) water

310 ml (10 fl oz/1¼ cups) cider vinegar

2 tablespoons salt

1 teaspoon ground cloves

1 teaspoon ground cinnamon

1 teaspoon ground allspice

1 teaspoon ground black pepper

In a large saucepan, cook cranberries, onions and water, covered, over low heat 30 minutes or until cranberries and onions are soft. Press through a sieve. Return juice to pan. Stir in sugar, vinegar, salt and spices. Cook over a low heat. Stir until sugar dissolves. Increase heat; bring to boil. Reduce heat; simmer 20 minutes.

Wash 5 (250 g/8 oz) jars in hot, soapy water; rinse. Keep hot until needed.

Ladle hot sauce into 1 hot jar at a time. Wipe rim of jar with a clean damp cloth. Cover. Fill and cover remaining jars. Sterilize 30 minutes in a water bath, page 93.

Makes 5 (250 g/8 oz).

Tomato Sauce

3.6 kg (8 lb.) ripe tomatoes, coarsely chopped

8 large onions, coarsely chopped

900 g (2 lb./4 cups) demerara sugar

1.1 l (2 pt/5 cups) sugar

6 tablespoons black peppercorns

3 tablespoons salt

1 teaspoon ground cloves

1 teaspoon cayenne pepper

In a large saucepan, simmer all ingredients 2 hours. Stir occasionally. Strain through a sieve. In a large saucepan, bring purée to a boil. Boil 5 minutes.

Wash 7 (250 g/8 oz) jars in hot, soapy water; rinse. Keep hot until needed.

Ladle hot sauce into 1 hot jar at a time. Wipe rim of jar with a clean damp cloth. Cover. Fill and cover remaining jars. Sterilize 30 minutes in a water bath, page 93.

Makes 7 (250 g/8 oz).

Plum Sauce

1 kg (2 lb.) plums, coarsely chopped

250 g (8 oz/1¼ cups) sugar

600 ml (1 pt/2½ cups) vinegar

1 teaspoon salt

1 teaspoon ground ginger

½ teaspoon cayenne pepper

¼ teaspoon ground cloves

In a large saucepan, cook plums and stones over low heat 10 minutes. Add remaining ingredients. Increase heat; bring to a boil. Reduce heat; simmer 30 minutes. Press through a sieve. Return juice to pan. Cook over low heat 30 minutes. Stir occasionally.

Wash 5 (250 g/8 oz) jars in hot, soapy water; rinse. Keep hot until needed.

Ladle hot sauce into 1 hot jar at a time. Wipe rim of jar with a clean damp cloth. Cover. Fill and cover remaining jars. Sterilize 30 minutes in a water bath, page 93.

Makes 5 (250 g/8 oz).

FRUIT IN ALCOHOL

Fruit in alcohol improves when kept, so allow the fruit to mellow at least one month before serving. The fruit will keep for one year. Serve as a dessert with cream or yoghurt or add to a fresh fruit salad.

Prepare fresh, high quality ripe fruit according to recipe. Prepare spices.

Place fruit, spices and sugar in clean, hot jars. Pour wine, brandy or rum over fruit; top up with water. Put on tops of jars, but not screwbands.

Place jars in 130C (250F) oven and leave for 3 hours. Remove from oven and screw on tops tightly. Cool and store.

Mulled Pears in Red Wine

2.7 kg (6 lb.) small, unripe pears

450 g (1 lb./2¼ cups) sugar

Peel of 1 lemon, cut in thin strips

1 bottle red wine

1 teaspoon whole cloves

1 (15-cm/6-in) cinnamon stick, cut in pieces

4 blades of mace

2 (8-cm/3-in) pieces of ginger root, bruised

Water

Wash 5 (1 l/35 fl oz) jars and lids in hot soapy water; rinse. Keep hot until needed.

Carefully peel whole pears retaining stalks. Pack into prepared jars. Divide sugar among jars.

Place a strip of lemon peel into each jar, and divide cloves, cinnamon stick, mace blades and ginger between jars. Pour wine over pears and top up jars with water. Put on tops of the jars but not screwbands. Place in 130C (250F) oven and leave for 3 hours. Remove from oven and screw on tops tightly. Cool and store.

Makes 5 (1 l/35 fl oz).

Brandied Apricots

2.7 kg (6 lb.) ripe apricots, peeled

1.8 kg (4 lb./9 cups) sugar

1.4 l (2½ pt/6¼ cups) water

Brandy

Wash 6 (450 g/16 oz) jars and lids in hot, soapy water; rinse. Keep hot until needed.

In a large saucepan, cook sugar and water over low heat. Stir until sugar dissolves. Increase heat; bring to a boil. Boil 10 minutes without stirring. Add apricots to syrup a few at a time. Reduce heat; simmer 5 minutes until apricots are soft but not broken. Using a slotted spoon, pack apricots into a hot warm jar. Simmer syrup until syrup resembles thin cream. Measure syrup. Measure an equal amount of brandy. Return syrup to pan. Increase heat; bring to a boil.

Remove from heat. Stir in brandy. Ladle syrup over apricots. Cover tightly.

VARIATION: Substitute peaches for apricots.

Makes 6 (450 g/16 oz).

Everlasting Rumpot

Mixed fruit, (strawberries, cherries, apricots, peaches, raspberries, plums, redcurrants, grapes or melon)

Sugar, equal to weight of fruit

Light or dark rum

Wash a jar or jars and lid or lids in hot, soapy water; rinse.

Do not use citrus fruit, apples, pears or bananas. Use sound ripe fruit, just a few pieces of each type, and wipe fruit gently. Do not wash, peel or remove stones from fruit. Only melon should be peeled, seeded and cut in large chunks. Layer fruit and sugar in prepared jar. Stir lightly. Pour rum over fruit to cover. Seal jar tightly.

Let mature in cool dark place 3 months. The Rumpot can be added to as more fruit becomes available. Always add equivalent sugar and more rum, if necessary, to keep fruit covered.

Serve with cream or yoghourt, add to fresh fruit salad, or use to fill hollowed-out melon, or flan case.

LIQUEURS

A liqueur is a sweetened alcoholic beverage flavoured with fruit or aromatics. Serve in liqueur glasses as an after-dinner drink or use as a sauce for ice cream or other dessert. Use drained fruit as a dessert with cream.

Prepare fruit or fruit juice according to recipe. Add sugar and flavourings.

Cook fruit juice and sugar according to recipe. Ladle into prepared jar or bottle.

Fill jar or bottle with spirits, such as brandy, rum, gin or vodka. Cover tightly. Let mature for 3 to 12 weeks, according to recipe. Shake jar occasionally. Filter liqueur into clean bottle. Seal tightly.

Orange Shrub

600 ml (1 pt/2½ cups) fresh orange juice, strained

900 g (2 lb./4½ cups) sugar

1 l (1¾ pt/4½ cups) light rum

Wash a large jar and lid in hot, soapy water; rinse. In a large saucepan, cook orange juice and sugar over low heat. Stir until sugar dissolves. Increase heat; boil 5 minutes, skimming off foam occasionally. Remove from heat; cool. Combine syrup and rum in prepared jar. Seal jar tightly. Let mature 2 weeks. Shake jar well each day. Let mature 4 weeks without disturbing. Filter liquid into 5 clean 250 ml/8 fl oz bottles. Seal tightly.

Makes 5 (250 ml/8 fl oz).

Cherry Brandy

450 g (1 lb.) Morello cherries

2 whole cloves

125 g (4 oz/½ cup) sugar

Approximately 850 ml (1½ pts/ 4 cups) brandy

Stone 10 cherries; crack the stones and remove kernels.

Wash a large jar and lid in hot, soapy water; rinse. Pack cherries and kernels into prepared jar. Add cloves, sugar and brandy. Seal jar tightly.

Let mature 12 weeks. Shake jar occasionally. Pour brandy into 4 clean 450 ml (16 fl oz) bottles. Seal tightly.

Makes 2 (450 ml/16 fl oz).

Coffee Liqueur

250 g (8 oz/1⅓ cups) dark brown sugar

150 ml (5 fl oz/⅔ cup) water

2 tablespoons instant coffee powder

600 ml (1 pt/2½ cups) brandy

Wash a large jar and lid in hot, soapy water; rinse. In a large saucepan, cook sugar and water over low heat 5 minutes. Skim off foam if necessary. Add coffee. Stir well; cool. Pour into prepared jar. Add brandy. Seal jar tightly.

Let mature 1 week. Shake bottle each day. Filter liquid into 2 clean (450 ml/16 fl oz) bottles. Seal tightly.

Makes 2 (450 ml/16 fl oz).

SYRUPS

Syrups are a thick solution of fruit juice, sugar and water. They can be made from soft fruits or tangy citrus fruits. Use over pancakes, biscuits or waffles, dilute with water as a drink or serve as a sauce with dessert.

Use clean ripe fruit. Wipe fruit instead of washing. If required remove peel in long strips.

If required squeeze juice from fruit. In a large saucepan, cook fruit or juice over low heat. Crush fruit several times. Strain through a jelly bag 12 hours. In a large saucepan cook juice, sugar and water. Use 375 g (12 oz/1½ cups) sugar for each 600 ml (1 pt./2½ cups) juice. Stir sugar until dissolved. Continue cooking according to recipe directions.

Pour into hot, sterilized bottles. Cover tightly with clean lids. Place a pad of thick paper in a large saucepan. Release tops ½ turn. Surround with boiling water, return to the boil, boil gently 30 minutes. Remove bottles. Tighten tops immediately.

Blackcurrant Syrup

2.7 kg (6 lb.) blackcurrants, stems removed

600 ml (1 pt/2½ cups) water

Sugar

Wash 5 (250 ml/8 fl oz) bottles and lids in hot, soapy water; rinse. Keep hot until needed.

In a large saucepan, simmer blackcurrants and water over low heat 1 hour. Crush blackcurrants several times. Strain through a jelly bag 12 hours. Measure juice. Measure 375g (12 oz/1½ cups) sugar for each 600 ml (1 pt/2½ cups) juice. In a saucepan stir sugar into juice over a low heat. Stir until sugar dissolves. Increase heat; bring to boil without stirring.

Strain hot syrup into 1 hot bottle at a time, leaving 1.5-cm (½-in) headspace. Wipe rim of bottle with a clean damp cloth. Cover. Fill and cover remaining bottles. Place on a pad of thick water in a saucepan. Release lids ½ turn. Surround with boiling water; 30 minutes. Remove bottles. Tighten lids immediately.

Makes 5 (250 ml/8 fl oz).

Raspberry Syrup

1.8 kg (4 lb.) raspberries

Sugar

Water

Place raspberries in a jelly bag. Squeeze to extract juice. Measure juice. Measure 375 g (12 oz/1½ cups) sugar and 600 ml (1 pt/2½ cups) water for each 600 ml (1 pt/2½ cups) juice. In a large saucepan, cook sugar and water over low heat. Stir until sugar dissolves. Add juice. Increase heat; bring to boil. Reduce heat; simmer 1 hour. Remove from heat; cool completely.

Wash 5 (250 ml/8 fl oz) bottles and lids in hot, soapy water; rinse. Keep hot until needed.

Pour cold syrup into 1 hot bottle at a time, leaving 1.5-cm (½-in) headspace. Wipe rim of bottle with a clean damp cloth. Cover. Fill and cover remaining bottles. Place on a pad of thick paper in a saucepan. Release lids ½ turn. Surround with boiling water; return to a boil; boil gently, 30 minutes. Remove bottles. Tighten lids immediately. Or pour cold syrup into clean freezer containers leaving 1.5-cm (½-in.) headspace. Attach lid. Store in freezer up to 12 months.

Makes 5 (250 ml/8 fl oz).

Orange Syrup

Peel of 6 Valencia oranges, cut in strips

900 g (2 lb./4½ cups) sugar

1 l (35 fl oz/4½ cups) water

600 ml (1 pt/2½ cups) fresh orange juice

2 tablespoons citric acid

In a large saucepan, cook orange peel strips, sugar and water over a low heat. Stir until sugar dissolves. Increase heat; boil 3 minutes. Remove from heat; cool. Strain through a jelly bag 12 hours. Add orange juice and citric acid. Mix well.

Wash 5 (450 ml/16 fl oz) bottles and lids in hot, soapy water; rinse. Keep hot until needed.

Pour hot syrup into 1 hot bottle at a time, leaving 1.5-cm (½-in.) headspace. Wipe rim of bottle with a clean damp cloth. Cover. Fill and cover remaining bottles. Place on a pad of thick paper in a saucepan. Release lids ½ turn. Surround with boiling water. Return to a boil; boil gently 30 minutes. Remove bottles. Tighten lids immediately.

Makes 5 (450 ml/16 fl oz).

FLAVOURED VINEGARS

Flavoured vinegars may be added to salad dressings and mayonnaise or used in pickles and sauces. Mix vinegar in glass, enamel or stainless steel bowls. Store in glass bottles or jars with a cork or vinegar-proof tops.

Place herbs or other flavouring material in a sterilized jar.

Fill jar with wine vinegar or cider vinegar. Seal tightly. Let stand 2 weeks.

Strain through a jelly bag or muslin. Add a little flavouring material, such as a sprig of tarragon, for an attractive appearance, if desired. Seal tightly.

Citron Vinegar

2 lemons

Grated peel of ½ orange

Grated peel and juice of 2 limes

1 l (1¾ ml/4½ cups) white wine vinegar

Pinch of salt

Pinch of paprika

Strips of lemon peel, to finish

Slice 1 lemon crosswise. Thread on a wooden skewer; grate peel of remaining lemon. In a large saucepan, bring skewer of lemons, lemon and orange peel, lime peel and juice, vinegar, salt and paprika to a boil. Remove from heat; cool completely. Transfer to a sterilized jar. Seal tightly with vinegar-proof lid. Let stand on a sunny or warm windowsill 2 weeks. Strain through a jelly bag.

Wash 5 (250 ml/8 fl oz) jars or bottles and lids in hot soapy water; rinse. Sterilize in boiling water.

Place strips of lemon peel in prepared jars or bottles. Pour vinegar into jars or bottles. Wipe rim of jars or bottles with a clean damp cloth. Seal tightly with vinegar-proof lids.

Makes 5 (250 ml/8 fl oz).

Raspberry Vinegar

1 kg (2 lb.) raspberries

1.1 l (2 pts/5 cups) red or white wine vinegar

Sugar

In a large bowl, cover raspberries with vinegar. Cover with a cloth. Let stand in a cool place 4 days. Strain through a jelly bag. Press fruit lightly. Measure juice. Measure 125 g (4 oz/½ cup) sugar for each 600 ml (1 pt/2½ cups) juice. In a medium saucepan, cook juice and sugar over low heat 15 minutes. Strain through a jelly bag.

Wash 5 (250 ml/8 fl oz) jars or bottles and vinegar-proof lids in hot, soapy water; rinse. Sterilize in boiling water.

Pour vinegar into prepared jars or bottles. Wipe rims of jars or bottles with a clean damp cloth. Seal tightly with vinegar-proof lids.

Makes 5 (250 ml/8 fl oz).

Herb Vinegar

**60 g (2 oz/1 cup loosely packed) fresh herbs, such as tarragon,
basil, marjoram, thyme, fennel or mint**

450 ml (16 fl oz/2 cups) white wine vinegar

1 fresh herb sprig

Place herbs in a sterilized jar. Fill with vinegar. Seal tightly with
vinegar-proof lid. Let stand 2 weeks. Strain through a jelly bag.

   Wash 1 (450 ml/16 fl oz) jar or bottle and a vinegar-proof lid in hot,
soapy water; rinse. Sterilize in boiling water.

   Place a fresh herb sprig in prepared jar or bottle. Pour flavoured
vinegar into jar or bottle. Wipe rim of jar or bottle with a clean damp
cloth. Seal tightly with a vinegar-proof lid.

Makes 1 (450 ml/16 fl oz).

MUSTARDS

Mustard is a pungent condiment. Serve in small quantities with cheese, meats and poultry or add to sauces and salad dressings. Mustard can be prepared from crushed mustard seeds or mustard powder, see Aromatic Mustard Powder page 117.

Soak mustard seeds in lukewarm water 12 hours if a smooth result is required.

Crush seeds with a wooden spoon, in a mortar and pestle, in a food processor/blender or in a coffee grinder.

Mix crushed seeds with vinegar and chosen herbs, spices, salt and pepper as specified in recipe. Pack into sterilized jars. Seal tightly. Let mature several days before using.

Aromatic Mustard Powder

450 g (1 lb/4 cups) mustard powder

125 g (4 oz/1 cup) salt

1 tablespoon garlic powder

1 tablespoon dried thyme, crushed

1 tablespoon dried tarragon, crushed

1 tablespoon powdered mixed spice

In a small bowl mix mustard powder and salt until evenly coloured. Stir in garlic powder, thyme, tarragon and mixed spice. Spoon in to clean jars. Seal tightly.

To use, mix with water or vinegar, or add 1 to 2 pinches to soup and stews.

Makes 3 (250 g/8 oz).

Extra Strong Mustard

4 tablespoons white mustard seeds

½ teaspoon ground nutmeg

½ teaspoon grated horseradish

¼ teaspoon ground allspice

8 tablespoons white wine vinegar

Salt and pepper

In a food processor/blender or a coffee grinder, crush mustard seeds. In a small saucepan cook mustard seeds with nutmeg, horseradish, allspice and vinegar over low heat 5 minutes or until thick and creamy. Cool completely. Add salt and pepper to taste. Spoon into a sterilized jar. Seal tightly.

Let mature 1 week before using.

Makes 8 tablespoons.

Household Mustard

310 ml (10 fl oz/1¼ cups) water

2 teaspoons sea salt

4 tablespoons white mustard seeds

8 tablespoons white wine vinegar

Salt and pepper

In a small saucepan, boil water and sea salt. Remove from heat. Let stand until lukewarm. In a medium bowl, pour salt water over mustard seeds. Let stand 12 hours, drain. Using a wooden spoon, crush seeds until soft and creamy.

In a small saucepan, bring vinegar to a boil. Gradually add to mustard. Add salt and pepper to taste. Spoon into a clean jar. Cover tightly.

Let mature several days before using. Will keep up to 1 month.

Makes 1 (250 g/8 oz).

CANDIED FRUITS

Candied fruit is a confection which may be eaten as a sweet or used in cakes and desserts.
Do not hurry candying, it is important to allow the fruit to become saturated in the sugar syrup over several days, or the fruit will be tough and wrinkled.

Fruit should be fresh and of high quality without blemishes. Prepare fruit by halving or slicing. Prepare syrup by dissolving sugar in water over low heat. Allow 310 ml (10 fl oz/1¼ cups) water to 185 g (6 oz/¾ cup) sugar for each 450 g (1lb.) fruit.

Simmer fruit in syrup. Let stand according to recipe. Repeat process for up to 7 days until fruit has absorbed all liquid.

Arrange fruit in a single layer; dry in a sunny or warm place 4 to 5 days, turning fruit occasionally until fruit is firm but not dry. Store in an airtight container.

Candied Chestnuts

1 kg (2 lb.) chestnuts, shells removed

900 g (2 lb./4 cups) sugar

600 ml (1 pt/2½ cups) water

1 vanilla pod

In a large saucepan, cover chestnuts with water. Bring to a boil; boil 8 minutes. Discard liquid. Drain. Using a kitchen towel, rub off brown inner skins. In a large saucepan, cook sugar, water and vanilla pod over low heat. Stir until sugar dissolves. Simmer 5 minutes. Add chestnuts. Increase heat; boil 10 minutes. Remove vanilla pod. Pour syrup and nuts into a large bowl. Let stand 12 hours. Return to pan. Boil 1 minute. Return to bowl. Let stand 24 hours. Repeat process 3 times until syrup has been absorbed.

Preheat oven to 65C (150F). Cover a wire rack with greaseproof paper. Place chestnuts on wire rack. Place in oven with oven door open 2 hours or until firm. Remove from oven; cool.

Store in a container lined with greaseproof paper. Will keep up to 2 weeks.

Makes 900 g/2 lb.

Candied Peel

Peel of 2 oranges

Peel of 2 lemons

220 g (7 oz/1 cup) sugar

In a large saucepan, cover peel with water. Cook over low heat 1½ hours. Add more water if necessary. Add sugar. Stir until sugar dissolves. Increase heat; bring to a boil. Remove from heat. Let stand 12 hours. Bring to a boil. Reduce heat; simmer 5 minutes. Remove from heat. Let stand 12 hours. Bring to a boil. Reduce heat; simmer until peel has absorbed nearly all of syrup. Drain peel.

Preheat oven to 65C (150F). Cover a wire rack with greaseproof paper. Place peel wire rack. Spoon a small amount of surplus syrup into centre of each piece of peel. Cover loosely with greaseproof paper. Place in oven with oven door open about 1 hour or until peel is firm and sugar crystallized. Remove from oven. Cool.

Store in an airtight container.

Candied Apricots

2 kg (4 lb./8 cups) sugar

600 ml (1 pt/2½ cups) water

1.8 kg (4 lb.) just-ripe apricots

Carefully skin at top of each apricot, squeeze out stones. In a large saucepan, cook sugar and water over low heat. Stir until sugar dissolves. Simmer 5 minutes. Add apricots. Increase heat; bring to a boil. Remove from heat. Let stand 1 hour. Bring to a boil again. Let stand 1 hour. Repeat process 3 times.

In a large bowl, let fruit and syrup stand 12 hours. In a large saucepan, boil fruit and syrup 1 minute. Drain fruit. Boil syrup; pour over fruit. Let stand 12 hours. Repeat this process twice until apricots are saturated and syrup is absorbed.

Cover a wire rack with greaseproof paper. Dry apricots on wire rack. Turn fruit occasionally until firm.

Store in an airtight container. Will keep up to 3 months.

Makes 1.8 kg (4 lb.)

DRYING

Drying fruit, vegetables and herbs produces a product which is relatively free from moisture. Add dried products to casseroles and stews or serve fruit as a dessert with cream. Dried herbs have a stronger flavour than fresh and should be used sparingly.

Use fresh ripe fruit or firm vegetables. If using apples and pears, drop into cold salted water. Use 1 tablespoon salt to every 1 l (¾ pt/4½ cups) water to prevent discolouration. Vegetables do not need soaking. Slice if necessary.

Spread in a single layer on oven or wire racks.

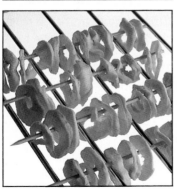

Dry in a 50 to 65C (120 to 150F) oven. Leave oven door slightly open so that air circulates and carries away moisture. Fruit should be soft, leathery and uncoloured. Vegetables should be crisp and firm. Let stand at room temperature 12 hours. Store in airtight containers. Will keep up to 1 year.

Dried Herbs

Mint, tarragon, thyme, sage, basil, marjoram

Preheat oven to 50 to 60C (120C to 150F). Divide herbs in small bunches. Spread on baking sheets in thin layers. Place in preheated oven 45 minutes until crisp and dry. Remove from oven. Let stand 12 hours.

Remove stems; rub herbs lightly with hands to break up leaves. Store in airtight container in a cool dark place. Label carefully; dried herbs can look very similar. Use within 4 to 6 months.

Dried Onions or Leeks

Onions or Leeks, as available

Cover oven racks with muslin. Preheat oven to 65C (150F).

If using onions, peel and remove any soft parts. Slice thinly crosswise; place on oven racks. If using leeks, strip off outer leaves. Slice crosswise in rings or cut into narrow lengthwise strips. Place on oven racks.

Place in oven 1 hour or until firm and crisp. Rearrange pieces several times to dry evenly.

Remove from oven. Let stand 12 hours. Store in airtight container.
To use, soak 15 minutes in cold water.

Dried Apple Rings

Firm, ripe apples, as available, peeled, cored.

Weak brine (2 tablespoons salt; 2.65 l (4¾ / 11¾ cups) water)

Preheat oven to 65C (150F). Slice apples into 10-cm (4-in) thick rings. In a large bowl, just cover apple rings with brine. Let stand 10 minutes. Drain apple rings; thread on wooden skewers.

Place skewers on oven shelves so apple rings do not touch. Place in oven 4 to 5 hours or until apple rings resemble soft leather and are moist and pliable.

Remove from oven. Let stand 12 hours. Store in airtight containers in a cool dry place.

To use, soak in fresh water 24 hours. In a medium saucepan, cook apples and liquid over low heat with a few strips of lemon peel, vanilla pod or a pinch of ground cloves.